Shoreline, WA **98133**
(415) 368-**3667**

Homeless:
A Day In The Life.

Todd Murphy

Copyright, 2018 by Todd R. Murphy

Any resemblance of any person described in this text to any actual person, living or dead, is purely coincidental.

All rights reserved. No part of this work may be reproduced in any form or by any electronic or mechanical means, including information storage or retrieval systems, without permission from the author, except by a reviewer who may quote brief passages in a review.

Public domain back cover image ('In Between the Glamour') by Kenny Louie (B.C., Canada)

First CreateSpace Edition.

Cover image from Paid Graphic service.

Murphy, Todd Raymond

"Homeless: A Day In The Life" / Todd R. Murphy – 1st Edition.

1) homelessness 2) poverty 3) sociology

Printed in the United States of America

1st of May, 2018 (Rev.4, 12.21.2018)

ISBN-13: 978-1987763119
ISBN-10: 1987763114

Visit us online here:
https://homelessadayinthelife.wordpress.com/

Or here:
www.facebook.com/homelessadayinthelife/

DEDICATION:

This book is dedicated to Karmu, Doris DeOme, Father +Nazarin, Pastor Bob, George Olebar, Negash Atsbeha, and Bhakti Dina Dayal Das, whose lofty thoughts inspired them to help the homeless. They were all of very different faiths and were of service in different ways, but each gave of themselves to help those who are the worst off in our country today. It's also dedicated to my friend Seth, who let me stay in his spare room, providing me with an address and a phone that helped me find a job, ending my own time as a homeless man, now so long ago.

CONTENTS

	Acknowledgments	vii
	Author's Preface	Pg. 9
1	Chapter One	Pg. 11
2	Chapter Two	Pg. 31
3	Chapter Three	Pg. 63
4	Chapter Four	Pg. 89
5	Chapter Five	Pg. 115
6	Chapter Six	Pg. 147
7	Chapter Seven	Pg. 171
8	Chapter Eight	Pg. 185
9	About the Author	Pg. 199

ACKNOWLEDGMENTS

Thanks are due to Father +Nazarin[1], who gave shelter, food, and showers to hobos and bums in his home for decades, for his help and encouragement in writing this book. Father +Nazarin was also once homeless, and raised himself up to become a clergyman who eventually sat with both beggars and kings.

NOTE TO READERS:

Like all books, this one has been edited many times, and there may be a few typos left in the text. If you find any, please point them out.

To send your comments, please use the feedback form here:

https://tinyurl.com/homelessbook

Many thanks from the author.

---

[1] Assyrian Orthodox Catholic Church, Syro-Chaldean Synod. Nestorian Patriarchal Jurisdiction.

Todd Murphy

AUTHOR'S PREFACE

I was homeless for 2 ½ years. It was rough, but I was young. During that time, I learned the ways of bums, beggars and hobos. I saw that there was no such thing as a typical homeless person. Some of them slept in shelters, and others didn't. Some drank or used hard drugs, while others stayed away from them. Some did nothing but panhandle (beg), while others lived only from trash picking. There were also those that collected bottles and cans to redeem them for the deposit. Not all were mentally ill, but nobody was well-adjusted.

Nearly everything I write about here was something I experienced myself. I sat on the ground with a begging sign; I searched through the garbage for anything I could find to sell. I was never a thief, though. I was always too afraid that I'd get caught. Eventually, I got a job while I was sleeping in someone's spare room. They let me use their address and phone number to apply for jobs. One of them, paying only minimum wage, came through.

The homeless are as varied in their ways of life as any other group. Some former homeless people may read this book and think that this isn't how it was for them, and they probably aren't wrong. There are many ways to survive on the street, and I didn't use them all.

Our main character, a fictitious homeless veteran, has no name. I could never think of one that seemed right, so we'll just call him "our friend." But then, nobody remembers the names of derelicts and beggars.

Homeless: A Day in The Life.

CHAPTER ONE

His bedroom was a patch of ground in a small park in the center of the city, unless someone else got there first. Then he had to find somewhere else to sleep.

He awoke to the noise of a garbage truck emptying out a dumpster, just a few yards away from him. The loud metallic booming sound from the garbage truck was enough to rouse him to consciousness, and the sound of the dumpster slamming back onto the pavement a few seconds later made it final. He was awake. His first thought was to remember how much money he had; one dollar and twenty cents. His mental inventory had bad news. He had no tobacco, no marijuana, and nothing to eat. Sitting up, trying to find an optimistic thought, it occurred to him that he didn't owe anyone any money.

Last night was chilly, but not cold enough for it to be safe to sleep out of the wind. When it's really freezing out, you can get away with sleeping someplace out of the way, like behind a dumpster, in a doorway, in an alley, or behind some bushes. That was nice. It was slightly warmer and gave you a little privacy. You could even go through your backpack, and arrange your things without anyone watching. The "bum bashers," who liked to beat up homeless people, didn't come out when it was really cold. Our friend had seen too many people begging for change or pushing shopping carts filled with bottles and cans, with their faces marked with scabs and bruises, the result of nighttime beatings, to ignore the risk.

You're asking for trouble if you sleep someplace out of the way when it's warm. You could end up covered in bruises or worse if the bum bashers found you. Besides that, the cops are more likely to hassle you when you sleep in a secluded spot. They'll force you to move somewhere else because they don't want to find you beaten up and lying behind a bush. If that happens, they'll have to call for an ambulance, get you to a hospital, and write an incident report. And after all that was done, you might not show up in court to testify against the guys who tried to pound your face in. The police don't like to deal with this kind of thing if they can help it. A lot of the homeless victims they found tried to refuse their help. Most of these beatings brought nothing worse than a slew of cuts and bruises, and in those cases, the homeless were afraid that they'd spend hours waiting for the same treatment that they could get for themselves. A few Band-Aids was often all they needed, and if they could get those themselves, then why put up with the ordeal of waiting for hours in the emergency room to get them? The ER staff had been through too many difficult nights with homeless people, brought in against their will, arguing about everything. It made the nurses cranky, brusque, and short tempered. The police would insist that the victims of such beatings see a doctor, and they pretty much had to go along with them. The emergency room is a hard place to be at 2:00 AM, with its bright lights, policies against smoking and drinking, and short tempered nurses. They wouldn't let you sleep on the floor, either. Still, the ER was a lot better than a jail cell, even if you were only there for a few hours.

These small violent gangs of "bum bashers" could be merciless, and for some reason, they seemed to take a special pleasure in opening your backpack and scattering your things all over, just to show that they could. When it happens, you sit there and say inane things like "But I didn't do anything to you guys" or "Why are you doing this"? There's no response to this kind of lunacy, except to wish that it would stop. You can beg for mercy, but if they had any, you wouldn't need to beg for it in the first place. Cruelty doesn't have conversations.

They could get away with it. Cops would often believe the attackers more than their homeless victims, especially if they were drunk. There are police who aren't prejudiced against the homeless, but even they usually won't make an arrest unless they saw the beating for themselves. Otherwise, they'll just chase the muggers away, or let them go after a talking to, and tell you to pack up your stuff and move along. It's the only thing they ever want to do. There's no paperwork involved, and no key witness who might be too smashed to show up in court or to testify against their attackers.

There are several kinds of street predators the bums have to look out for. The bum bashers were only the most dangerous of them. There are groups of drunken young men in their twenties who, like high school bullies, got their thrills by tormenting the defenseless even after their school days were over.

They would ridicule and heckle homeless men until they got angry, and then run off. Their currency was humiliation, not pain, but they were still more than a little irritating. The danger they presented was that the homeless man would eventually strike back, committing *assault and battery*, a felony, while they themselves could only be charged with a misdemeanor, and for the cops, it was the gang's word against the bum's word. The homeless men couldn't win in these bizarre confrontations. It was hard for the cops to believe the homeless guy was telling the truth, and if he was, the police didn't care. Very few policeman will take it seriously if a homeless beggar says, "They're making fun of me." All the same, it could turn into a serious business. Almost anyone will get violent if you harass and provoke them long enough. Then, they go to jail, and their provocateurs have a good laugh.

Last night, our friend decided that it wasn't quite cold enough to sleep in a sheltered spot to try to get out of the wind. The gangs made it too risky. His shoulder ached from the odd strain of keeping his arm in the strap of his backpack while he was asleep; but he had to do it, to make sure he'd wake up if anyone tried to steal it. He only slept for five hours, through the very coldest hours of the night. It's just common sense. If you know you're less likely to get mugged sleeping in the open in the early (and cold) hours, you learn to stay awake until it's safe. Besides, he could always lie down for a couple hours later on. He never really slept in the middle of the day, but just resting could be almost as good as sleep. He hadn't slept more than five hours at a time for months, so he was tired all the time.

He slept in his clothes, so getting dressed in the morning just meant putting on his shoes. He rolled up his sleeping bag and strapped it to the bottom of his backpack.

The first order of business was to find a dumpster to piss behind, a cup of coffee, and a cigarette, or at least some tobacco. The pissing happened quickly. Nobody wanted to see a homeless man peeing next to a dumpster, but very few people were willing to talk to him while he was doing it, even to tell him "Don't do that here." And everybody seemed to know where the homeless aren't supposed to piss, but nobody could tell him where he *was* supposed to pee. He pulled the newspaper, which he used as insulation against the cold at night, out of his pants.

With only $1.20, he couldn't buy any tobacco or coffee. Coffee could be had for no less than $1.50 that time of day, and tobacco for no less than five dollars. He could manage without buying either. "Pre-owned" tobacco is a lot better than no tobacco, and secondhand coffee is better than none.

The only people out on the street at this hour are the ones on their way to work, or the ones whose work kept them outside. Because a lot of them light up a cigarette when they get off the bus, and then toss it down when they reach their office, the financial district was always good place to look for cigarette butts in the morning. Unless it was raining. He scanned the sidewalk for any worthwhile butts as he walked along, but only found one. It would be his first smoke of the day, and he lit it on the spot. Ecstasy.

After walking for about five or ten minutes, he reached the financial district, and started paying attention to the sidewalk around the entrances to office buildings. In a few minutes, he had amassed a collection of six cigarette butts, picked up over three blocks. Each one of them was either a half a cigarette, or maybe a little bit more. It was the actual equivalent of three or four cigarettes. Two of them had been stepped on and were pressed completely flat. He could tear the cigarette paper off of them and mix it up in his hands, and smoke it in his pipe, which bore the faint outline of a marijuana leaf.

Two of the butts were half a cigarette each, and they were in good condition. Together they would make a good morning smoke, but he would save that pleasure until he got some coffee to go with it. He had a paper coffee cup from 7-Eleven, which he took from the trash bin in front of the place the night before. The next step was to find the coffee. Food and drink were not allowed on the city buses, so people often left half full cups of coffee sitting by the bus stop, too lazy to put them in the trash. A half-full cup wasn't much to expect this time of day. He crossed the street and started walking back towards the park where he had slept the night before, now about seven blocks away. He checked every bus stop, but didn't see any today. After a couple of blocks, he began looking *inside* the trash cans, and soon found a large cup of Starbuck's, about half-empty, standing almost upright. Starbuck's likes to serve coffee in extravagantly large sizes with fancy Italian names, like "enorme", "monumentale", "grandioso", or "leviatano." Half a cup of Starbuck's coffee would almost fill the empty paper cup he scrounged the night before, conveniently bearing the logo for 7-Eleven.

He had $1.20, and bananas were 60¢ each at the 7-Eleven. So, his plan was feasible. He took the cold coffee from the Starbuck's cup, poured it into the 7-Eleven cup, and then carried it to the nearest 7-Eleven, just two blocks away. He walked in, smiled and nodded to the turbaned Indian clerk, who never seemed to notice anything he didn't have to, and made sure the clerk saw that he was carrying the coffee *into* the store, so it was already paid for. He put his 7-Eleven coffee into the microwave oven and pressed for one minute. While his coffee was heating, he ambled around the shop pretending he was deciding what to buy. When the bell rang, he got his coffee, went to the counter, and paid for his banana, which made him an actual 'customer,' and justified using their microwave. The clerk had no way of knowing that the coffee wasn't theirs, and probably wouldn't care. One of the other guys who worked the front counter was a real prick with a special loathing for homeless men. He loved to remind them that he barely tolerated them, and that he could throw them out of the store at any moment. The microwave trick worked with him too, but he still made our friend nervous.

Now he had his morning coffee, his first cigarette of

the day, and a banana. He didn't really want it; he didn't like eating first thing in the morning, but the banana cost 60¢ and a fresh cup of coffee would've cost $1.60, so he'd saved a dollar. He would've had to panhandle 40¢ before he could buy a cup of coffee outright, so this was easier.

Congratulating himself for having the willpower not to light up one of his cigarette butts as soon as he found it, he looked forward to sitting down and enjoying his breakfast. He decided to eat the banana. His backpack was so full that if he put it away, it would probably get squashed.

Finding a place to sit down wasn't difficult, but it wasn't something you could take for granted, since the city had removed all the benches, and office buildings now had strips of spiked metal on the outside of their first-floor windowsills, so you couldn't sit on them.

He hoped that there would be an open table when he got back to the park. If not, there were still benches there. When he reached the place, he found most of the tables were being used, so he sat down on a bench.

It would feel better if he lit his cigarette butts last, so he opened the banana, and after a few bites, started to feel a little nauseous. There was a reason he didn't like to eat first thing in the morning. He left what remained of it on top of a trash bin, in case another homeless person was hungry. He also took a slight, but almost spiritual pleasure in leaving food for the homeless, even though he was homeless, too.

He took a sip from his coffee, and knew that whatever Starbuck's patron had so generously put it in the trash where he could find it, liked theirs without sugar. For a moment, he was angry with himself for not thinking of taking a couple of sugar packets while he was at the 7-Eleven, but decided that the coffee was good enough the way it was. Whoever bought it used about the right amount of cream. He was contented.

He put the longest of the cigarette butts in his mouth and took out his lighter. He could see that it was low on fluid, and wouldn't last long. Nevertheless, he was able to light his cigarette butt just the way he liked to. That meant he puffed very lightly when he first applied the flame to the tobacco. Some people like to draw on it as deeply as they can, as if to display their lust for the Lady Nicotine, but he preferred to make his last as long as possible. He puffed on his cigarette and sipped his coffee, and at last started to think about what he would do next. He decided he would sit with his bowl and his cardboard sign, which today read, "Two dollars short of the minimum deposit for a Swiss bank account. Please help."

He learned a long time ago that signs that said things like "Homeless. Hungry. Need Help," might tell the truth, but they weren't what people wanted to see. Their minds couldn't fathom the difference between the flow of money in their lives and the economics of homelessness, and it didn't do any good to try to tell them. His sign that said, "Open source gigolo. Will work for cash." Brought in the more money, but also encouraged the wrong kind of people to stop and talk to him. He threw out the sign that said "Why lie? I need a beer" several days ago. It brought smiles (and, like all other begging signs, seemed to encourage some people to ignore him), but it really only pulled in money on Friday and Saturday nights, when there were a good number of drunk people around. The same drunken idiots who would beat him up for fun could also be happy to give him money to get him drunk. Thinking of this, he said "This world is fuckin' crazy" out loud.

The sweet dizziness of the first real smoke of the day swept through his body in a wave of pleasure that never comes in any other way. He closed his eyes so he could pay complete attention to the sensation. Coffee, tobacco, and a few mouthfuls of food, and for a moment, he was as happy as any prince having his breakfast.

Making his way back to the financial district, he sat down on the sidewalk, leaning against his backpack on a stretch of pavement that fell between the entrances to two office buildings. That meant there were no storefronts there and no shopkeeper to come out to complain and tell him to move on. He'd sat there before, and knew that probably no one would hassle him. Executives walked by with their briefcases, secretaries and clerical workers went by staring at their cell phones, and while it seemed that they looked at his sign, no one looked at him. After a while, he lit up another one of his cigarette butts, and puffed it slowly. A few coins fell in his bowl, and then a dollar bill. It wasn't enough. He'd have to stay longer than he expected to meet his goal of seven dollars. With five bucks, he could go back to the park and buy a small nugget, or "nug" of marijuana and a fresh coffee. The guy who sold it to him, a Rastafarian named Tate, wouldn't sell any less. For Tate, it was a mission. The smoke was a sacrament to "Jah," the God of his religion and he believed he was spreading a divine blessing by selling it, but he would never sell less than five dollars at a time, or give any credit. It was strictly cash and carry.

It took over two hours to make the seven dollars, enough for a nickel bag and a fresh cup of coffee, (with sugar), and a small cigar, if he added the $1.20 he already had. After stopping in a 7-Eleven to buy them, he headed back to the park, thinking that he hadn't done badly. The timing was right. If he'd stayed much longer, he would've been sitting on the sidewalk during the lunch break. Then it would be too crowded for anyone to notice him. It gets packed down there sometimes.

Fortunately, Tate was in his usual place and had a couple of nickel bags already prepared, so it only took a minute, including his rap about how we are all blessed, and what a wonderful world this is. Tate worked hard to keep a positive attitude, but he also had a room, and that made it easier. Our friend saw him angry a few times, but he never saw him depressed.

So now he had half a gram of marijuana, fresh coffee and a little cigar. He didn't especially like cigars, but they were easy to put out and light up again, and weren't as foul as cigarettes when you smoked them a second time. You could also buy just one. With cigarettes, you had to buy a whole pack.

He tore up one of his cigarette butts, and packed some tobacco into the bottom of his ganja pipe, the one with the faded pot leaf on it, then he took a little pot, crushed it in his fingers, and put it in the pipe. Next, he took a little more tobacco, and spread it over the top. Now, when he lit up, it would smell like tobacco as much as marijuana, and any passing policeman might not be completely sure what they were smelling. It made the pot last a lot longer than smoking it by itself. Noticing once again that his lighter was low on fluid, he lit his pipe, took a deep drag, and held the smoke in his lungs. He pressed his thumb over the bowl of the pipe to extinguish it, and as part of the same movement, slipped it back into his jacket pocket. That way, no passing policeman could see that he was smoking, after let his hit go. Once he exhaled, there would be no question about *what* someone was smoking. Putting the pipe in his pocket before the inevitable out breath made it hard for anyone to be sure *who* had been smoking. After a few strained coughs, his lungs recovered from the sudden onslaught well enough for him to light the little cigar, and he began to drink his coffee. Stoned.

He thought about going back to the financial district and sitting with his sign some more, but he also knew that he'd have to spend any money he earned that way almost immediately, so his cash reserves, still hovering at a little more than a dollar, wouldn't grow in the slightest.

"Time for a new venture." he said to himself.

He decided that when his coffee and the third of the cigar he would allow himself (saving what was left for later) were done, he'd go into the back alleys and check out the dumpsters. Trash picking was one of his main occupations. "You never know what you'll find."

People who live in apartment buildings are constantly throwing away useful things, along with their kitchen and bathroom trash, dirty diapers, bags of cat litter, bottles, cans, and untold plastic wrappers. The nice thing about trash from apartments is that you knew where it had been. With ordinary trash, thrown away by ordinary people, you can inspect the food and if it was good you could eat it. No one is out to poison you. If something smelled bad, you just left it alone.

One of the arts involved in being homeless is knowing where to sell the things you find in the trash. You could usually find someone to buy a stereo system, a television or an iPhone that you found in the street, but it's better if you know how to sell used clothing, old books, and jewelry. These things wound up in the trash far more often than expensive but obsolete electronics. You need to be an expert to look at a cell phone with a dead battery, to know what kind it is and how much you can get for it. There were enormous billboards all over downtown telling him what the newest version was, but the older ones were still worth something.

He paused to think about the fact that his identification card would expire in a few months, and even though he had an address where they could send the ID (at the homeless shelter), he'd still have to pay the fee. He got his passport before his life collapsed, and it was good for another three years. When you go to sell something to a store secondhand you'll get a lot more for it if you have an ID than if you don't. If you don't have one, people will assume that you stole whatever you're trying to sell, and you're only saying you don't have ID to avoid being caught.

You can go to a pawnshop with a solid gold class ring, but if you don't have ID, the buyer usually won't even look at it. If they do, they'll only offer a small fraction of what they'd pay to someone with one, which they photocopied whenever they bought something. It let them make a record of who sold it to them. Otherwise, they'll assume its "stolen property" and either stay away from it, or handle it "off the books."

"Hey man, you got an ID card?"

"No man, not me. Sorry."

He had to lie and tell the other street people that he didn't have an ID. If they knew he did, they'd keep asking him to go to the pawnshop, secondhand clothing shop, or used bookstore, and sell their things for them. He did that once, with a stack of college textbooks, but when he handed the money over to the guy who'd found them in the trash, the man got angry at our friend. And then, disappointed in how little the books had brought, and reneged on his promise to split the money. So he had taken a bus ride, paying the fare, and put in about two hours of his time for about six dollars. Better to sit in the street with a sign that says, "Give me money. Fuck you."

When he worked on his own, dumpster diving (trash picking) could be pretty good. The dumpsters were emptied once or twice a week. Dumpsters that were emptied several days ago were usually full, and you didn't have to reach in as far to get whatever was on the top. But they were more likely to have rotten, slimy food in them, which always smelled bad. If you get any on your clothes it either stayed there, or you cleaned it off by hand, unless you could manage to get your laundry done, or found another jacket. He really didn't want to find another one. The jacket he had was warm at night, and probably once cost a great deal of money. A warm jacket was a valuable resource. You have to be careful.

When he got to his first block for the day, flanked by apartment buildings, he started opening the dumpsters, and saw that the trash was just about perfect. It looked like it had been emptied two or three days before, so any food put in there just after it was last emptied probably wouldn't be foul enough to soil his clothes yet. It would probably be okay to climb in the dumpsters if there was anything in them worth taking. You could stink yourself up if you got into a trash bin with rotting food in it.

He didn't find much in the first couple of dumpsters.

He found a belt, but it was no better than the worn one he had on. He found a pair of pants that looked like they would fit him, but he already had a second pair in his backpack, and there was no room for a third. There was a paper bag filled with empty wrappers from snack foods, and incomprehensibly, a small unopened package of sliced turkey meat. It was still cold. He opened it on the spot, and ate it right there, standing next to the dumpster. He wished he still had the other half of his banana, or a piece of bread.

The next dumpster he opened had a strange treasure on the top. It was a grocery bag filled with several kinds of "Hello Kitty" toys, and they looked like they were brand-new. Some of them still had price tags. His intuition, honed through long experience pulling trash out of garbage bins, told him that this might be the best he was going to get that day. But then, you never know.

He knew what to do with it. This was a bag of stuff to sell in the street. No pawn shops, no secondhand stores, and no trying to barter them. There was also a tourist market in the area around the park and the financial district, filled with lots of small interesting shops. There was a store that only sold hand-dipped candles. Another that only carried old posters. Another sold movie memorabilia. There were dozens of restaurants, ethnic food shops and luxury gourmet emporia. There were also street musicians, jugglers, and balloon twisting artists. Foot traffic was heavy; there were plenty of people, and lots of families. He walked up and down the street in the thickest area waiting for his customer. It would be a family with a kid wearing a Hello Kitty T-shirt or backpack. Within a very few minutes, an Asian family came down the sidewalk with a young girl who fit the description. He let them pass him, and then turned around and followed them, keeping pace a couple of yards behind them. When they stopped at the next corner, he approached them from the side with the little girl and said:

"You like Hello Kitty?"

The little girl said yes, and he looked at her father, who was scowling at him, opened the bag so the man could see into it and said:

"I have some Hello Kitty toys here. Would you like to look at them? I need to sell them."

The father looked at him, a bit repulsed by his scruffy and abrupt appearance, but still only asked: "Are they stolen?"

He maneuvered himself in front of the family.

He answered, "No. I found them. Who would steal Hello Kitty dolls?" Without waiting for an answer, he took out the largest one and held it up. The young girl's eyes filled with an inner light that conveyed the sublime benediction Japanese pop culture offered to those with cuteness in their hearts (Harōkiti!). It was obvious that the father wanted them for his kid.

Our friend handed the bag to the kid's father, inviting

him to look over the merchandise. Once the father had it in his hand, they were half way to making a deal. The man dug through the bag for a moment, and saw they were clean and new.

"I'll prove they're not stolen. I'll let you name the price." Logic has no place in street negotiations.
<"Please Daddy." >
"I don't know how much to offer."
<"Please, please, Daddy.">
"Whatever you think is right."
"Hmm … . How about 20 dollars, okay?"

They certainly cost a lot more than that, but it didn't matter what they sell for in the store. For him, the important thing was how much he could get for them *now*, so he agreed. He might wind up carrying them around all day if he couldn't sell them. As they walked away, the child looked thrilled; the man looked smug, and his wife looked appalled.

'The very idea, buying toys for our child from a beggar in the street.' But he got the $20, the kid had a whole bunch of little Hello Kitty dolls, and anyone would know with the intuition of a dozen psychics, that no way was that kid ever going to get so many such high quality Hello Kitty toys all at once except maybe, just maybe, on their birthday, or perhaps Christmas.

So now, he had a little bit of marijuana, and about $22, and two thirds of a little cigar. He decided he would carry on dumpster diving, after he went to see Tate again, and got another nickel bag. That should be enough to last him into the middle of the next day. There was even still one good 'hit' left in the pipe in his pocket. He would smoke it soon.

Now it was time for food. The tourist market also had fruit and vegetable sellers, so he bought another banana and a plum for a $1.10, and then crossed the street to a Chinese bakery, where he bought two pork rolls for four dollars. That was more than enough to fill his stomach. Our friend looked in the trashcans as he went along, heading back to the park where he'd sit down to eat. He found a couple of handfuls of French fries in a paper tray, and thought he wouldn't take them, but he realized that they were still warm, so he ate a few of them on the spot. He also retrieved a plastic drinking water bottle, which he would fill at the water fountain in the park. The remaining French Fries went with him, too. Now he had some food, and a way to get something to drink.

It was still early.

Todd Murphy

Homeless: A Day in The Life.

CHAPTER TWO

So far, the day was going well. He was stoned, he'd had coffee twice, and looked forward to a good meal. The Hello Kitty toys were a stroke of good luck, not because it's so strange to find toys in the trash, or to find someone to buy something he'd found there, but because he'd taken it out of the trash and turned it into cash so quickly. The whole thing probably took about forty-five minutes.

Now he had about $17. He thought seriously about whether or not to buy tobacco, or hold onto the money and try and collect some more cigarette butts. He had two more. They'd been stepped on and squashed flat, but he could massage them back into the right shape. He decided on a compromise. He wouldn't buy a pack of cigarettes, and he wouldn't scrounge for butts anymore that day. Instead, he'd buy a pouch of Bugler tobacco, which comes with its own cigarette papers and roll his own. It's cheaper, and it isn't bad stuff, either.

He saw a lighter on the ground while he was eating, and picked it up, trying to light it. There was a spark, but no flame. Useless. After he finished eating, he lit one of his two cigarette butts, and allowed himself to inhale deeply, because he knew he'd buy more tobacco soon. He made short work of the remaining butt the same way. He packed his things up, and went to the tobacco store.

"Hey you, you don't make any trouble in my shop!"
"You get out of here!"

"What's the problem? I never make any trouble for you." He entered the shop as though he hadn't heard the owner telling him to leave, and put a five dollar bill on the counter, and said "A pack of Bugler tobacco, please."

At that point, it was easier for the shopkeeper to sell him the tobacco and let him leave on his own than it was to order him out. He was through the door again as soon as he had his tobacco. There was no point in asking why he was being thrown out of the store. He knew. He was homeless, and someone who looked like him had made trouble there before. Besides, the owner didn't like selling five-dollar packages of Bugler. He was really there to sell hundred dollar boxes of cigars, and homeless customers don't encourage the rich clientele.

The stench of his own sweat filled his nostrils as he reached into his jacket to put the tobacco in an inner pocket. There was no way around it. He stank. He didn't mind the smell himself very much, but he knew it bothered people, and there was only one solution. A fresh T-shirt and a bathroom, with a door that locked, where he could wash himself. He knew a couple of places. He could go to the shelter, even though he wouldn't sleep there, and wait in line, first to register at the front desk, and then again to get into the showers. While he was in there, he'd have to leave his backpack in the changing room he'd be sharing with several others.

He didn't like getting naked in front of anyone. It didn't matter that they were just as decrepit as him. The important thing was that they would be complete strangers, overseen by a "volunteer" doing community service as his sentence for one minor felony or another. It was humiliating. Besides that, having someone go through his pack, or just steal it outright, would've been catastrophic. Everything he owned in the world was in that bag.

One of the unwritten rules of living on the streets is that you never, never, mess with anyone's gear. If you saw an unattended backpack on the ground in a place where there are a lot of homeless people, you didn't touch it. The bag is only abandoned if it's been there for many hours, and there was always someone who lived more dangerously than he did, and was willing to take a chance and grab it first. Leaving your bag out of sight was usually a bad idea.

He tried sleeping in a shelter when he first became homeless, but it didn't work out at all. When he got there the first time, he read the list of rules posted just inside the door. One of the rules was that he had to be in there by 6 PM, and stay there until at least 7 AM the next morning. That meant that he had to sit on the cot they assigned him from six until the 11 o'clock 'lights out'. The first time he went there, he had arrived around 7:30, so he was too late. The volunteer at the desk was annoyed with him for not coming on time. He didn't seem to care when our friend told him that he didn't know the rules. "You *better* know the rules before you get here. We're here giving you a place to sleep, lettin' you get a shower, an' givin' you the chance to git out o' the col'." He asked if they had a copy of the rules he could take with him to study, but that just seem to irritate the guy even more. He read the rules posted on the wall, underneath a cracked plexiglass cover:

"Line up to receive a number when you arrive. We have only 75 beds. Sleeping on the floor is not allowed. No exceptions."
(This controlled the number of people in the shelter.)

"Cooperate with the staff."
(This really meant you had to do what you were told.)

"No alcohol, drugs or intoxication. Violators will have to leave, and may not return."
(This let some of the donors think that they were helping get people off of drugs.)

"Do not throw dirty clothing in the trash bins."
(Filthy underwear in the trash grossed the staff out.)

"Do not congregate in front of the building."
(This cut down on the number of complaints from their neighbors.)

"Smoking is strictly forbidden. No exceptions."
(This was a state law.)

"No weapons of any kind. No exceptions."
(The staff didn't want to get hurt, either.)

Homeless: A Day in The Life.

"We have a zero-tolerance policy for violence. Any violence, and we will call the police, and you will not be allowed to return."
(This let them throw people out when there was any kind of altercation, no matter how minor.)

"No food or drink in the sleeping room."
(It made a mess, and the homeless don't carry brooms.)

"Our doors open at 5 PM, and you must be out by 8 AM."
(By state law, if a homeless person could stay there all day, and they stayed longer than 30 days, they had "tenant rights", and couldn't be evicted without written notice, and possibly a court case. Getting everyone out, every day, ensured that the "guests" didn't become legal residents.)

"You may not use any blankets or sleeping bags, except those provided."
(Some of them had bedbugs from cheap hotels.)

"No noise. You may listen to music on your electronic device using headphones only."
(There had been fights over this, with some of them wanting to hear Hank Williams, while others wanted to listen to Hip-Hop.)

"No theft."
(Guaranteed to provoke fights, arguments and worse.)

"No pets."

(Fleas could be a problem.)

"Please respect your neighbors."
(This generic rule meant that almost any problem between two of the "guests" could get them both thrown out.)

"You may not wash articles of clothing in the bathroom sink."
(It got water all over the floor, and no one ever knew who did it.)

"We will not store your things for you." (They didn't have the space for it, and if they held a homeless man's bag for him, its owner would make a scene if there was any mistake when they returned it to him. Some would claim that something was missing and accuse one of the staff of stealing it.)

"If you leave the building after you have checked in, you may not return that night."
(This meant you couldn't leave the building and sell your ticket to someone who was on the forbidden list, or who just got there too late. You also couldn't go out, get drunk and come back in.)

"You can only use the showers after you check in at the front desk, and have your number."
(This kept the number of showers down. Hot water costs money.)

"You must allow our staff to inspect your bags and/or pockets when requested to do so. Refusals will result in your being asked to leave."

Homeless: A Day in The Life.

(This suspended all "search and seizure" laws while you were in the shelter. More than one homeless guy had stood, watching a volunteer search through his bag, while the cops stood by, looking at everything in it.)

It seemed like they only had one solution to any problem that came up, "being asked to leave." That was the phrase they always used, "being asked to leave." In fact, it wasn't a request; it was an order. If they asked you to leave, you *had* to go. "No exceptions." If you tried to refuse, you'd be guilty of trespassing; they would call the cops, and you'd get busted. If you asked to talk to the boss instead of just walking out as ordered, they could charge you with *disorderly conduct*. There was no appeal when one of the staff issued a command.

Disorderly conduct:
1) Actions that disturb others. 2) Minor criminal offenses, such as public drunkenness, loitering, or disturbing the peace, 3) Loud threats or 4) Parties loud enough to create a nuisance.

A clever cop could always find more charges. If you argued with the police, even in the slightest, you could have resisting arrest added to the charges. You don't actually have to fight with the cops to be charged with *resisting*.

Resisting Arrest:
A criminal charge against an individual who has committed, depending on the jurisdiction, at least one of the following acts:
1) Fleeing a police officer while being arrested. 2)

Threatening a police officer with physical violence while being arrested. 3) Physically struggling to free oneself from being restrained (handcuffed or put into the police vehicle). 4) Assaulting a police officer while being arrested (also known as assault). 5) Providing an officer with false identification (either verbally or by presentation of a false official document, i.e. a fake ID). 6) Any actions that prevent a police officer from conducting the arrest in an orderly fashion.

Just failing to cooperate with the cops and walking away can be enough to get that charge if they suspected you of something. *Cooperative* was a euphemism for *obedient*. After all, it was impossible to be disobedient and cooperative with them at the same time. In the street, the police didn't hit everyone who argued with them with a resisting arrest charge, but everybody knew they had that power. "Proceed at your own risk."

The homeless felt respected when they were left alone, while the police felt respected when they got obedience and compliance. If you refused to talk to the cops, even when you weren't a suspect, you could be charged with *interfering with police duties*

Interference With Police Duties
A person commits an offense if that person, with criminal negligence, interrupts, disrupts, impedes, or otherwise interferes with a peace officer while performing their duty or exercising an authority imposed or granted by law.

The shelters could be callous when someone stepped out of line. They expected you to be submissive and do what you were told. If they asked you to leave, you left. You had to be "orderly" at all times, though no one could tell you what that really means. In practice, it often meant whatever the staff wanted it to. Most cops didn't use the power that such a vague charge gave them. Arresting drunken homeless men was a hassle. It only created more paperwork, and the people they busted on such ambiguous charges were usually back on the street in no time. It was a waste of time and energy for all concerned.

The shelter's list of rules went on. Most of them looked like they were made up in response to past problems (somebody arrived with a dog that barks a lot, so they made a rule against that), or to satisfy their donors that their "guests" weren't taking drugs. He'd heard people talking about the shelters. Their stories always compared them to prisons.

There was always a "King Rat." He was the guy you went to if you had to leave after getting in and hoped to sneak back in later. That was against the rules. If you paid him enough (not much, really), he'd let you stash your backpack under his cot, and tell you how to knock on the emergency exit door, with its sabotaged alarm, close to his bed. When he heard the right knock, he'd let you in, unless one of the staff was in the room. In that case, you'd just have to wait.

You had to give him *something*. Cigarettes, cash, a beer, or anything else he could use. If they caught him, they'd throw him out, telling him never to return, though he might bribe one of the orderlies to get his name off the forbidden list. The King Rat could make

$20 or $30 in one night, but he usually took in a lot less. His reasoning was sound. He'd found a way to continue making money throughout the night. Most of the time, he could only collect five or ten bucks that way, but it was enough to get him started the next day, with some cigarettes, tobacco, coffee, or crack.

The shelter gave you coffee in the morning, but everyone agreed that it was the worst in the world. There was no point in asking for sugar or the powdered cream. If they were there, you used them. If not, you went without. Breakfast was always the same. A bowl of oatmeal and one slice of toast. You could stand a spoon in the oatmeal, and it would take a full fifteen seconds to fall over to the side. The director of the place, who seemed to believe in every detail of its operations, would enthusiastically tell their "guests" that they'd have a "hearty" breakfast in the morning.

The garbage cans were full of oatmeal when breakfast was over, at 7:45 AM precisely. It was just too damn thick. The men ate in silence, standing at the table, and drank the unspeakably bad coffee. There were no chairs, so no one would hang around after they finished eating. The watery brew was the only way to wash the oatmeal down. One of the jokes in the place was that the staff got their coffee from the 7-Eleven down the street 'cause they wouldn't drink the stuff either. The same for the oatmeal. The cooks would not eat what their hands had made.

At 7:55 AM, one of the staff would walk around

yelling, "Five *minutes*. Everybody out. I mean *now*." The staff would nag you mercilessly if you were late getting out or if you were still packing your gear when they closed up. More than one "guest" who tested their patience found themselves being grabbed and thrown out into the street, forced to abandon their possessions. The rules were absolute, and the enforcement could be merciless. Most of the staff were quietly impatient - about everything. The "guests" made jokes about Zyklon B in the shower. The place was like a concentration camp, and if the staff overheard you saying anything like that, they'd either ignore you or remind you that you were free to leave, and no one would force you to return.

In a city with thousands of homeless people, they could be as bossy as they wanted, and there would always be more people looking for beds than they could provide. That explained the rule about no sleeping on the floor. The sign said there were no exceptions, but on the coldest nights in winter, the police would bring in nearly frozen street people, and demand the shelter find more space for them. If the police asked for an exception to the rules, they got it. It was a homeless shelter, and they had complaints from nearby merchants and people who lived in the neighborhood. They needed friends at City Hall, so the city government trumped their system of rules. You could only sleep on the floor if the cops brought you in. When our friend asked why they made an exception when the police took in someone, but not when a homeless man asked, they'd say they didn't know either. "They don't tell me nuthin'." Some shelters were much better, like the ones for single mothers, but he didn't qualify. Wrong gender; no kid. He had no idea what they were like.

You had to wait in line to get to the front desk when you first arrived. The volunteer would ask you a few questions, including whether or not you were seriously ill. If you were, they wouldn't let you in, because they didn't want to take responsibility for your medical problems. "This isn't a hospital." They could get a van to take you to the emergency room, but the homeless could walk into the ER more easily than they could walk into the shelter, so there wasn't much point.

When you were finished at the front desk, you waited in line outside on the sidewalk, listening for them to call your name. If you left the line, you lost your bed for the night.

You might arrive and find no one waiting in line at the front desk. That happened when all the beds were assigned for the night, so you couldn't register, and you couldn't use the shower.

They would also take your thumbprint and your picture, so they'd have a photo to show the police if they came looking for you. They gave you a paper with a number and the date on it. That was the number of your bed for that one night. Somehow, no one knew exactly, the police could access their database, and get a picture of any of them. This helped the police to find suspects ("Have you seen this guy?").

The shelter would let anyone who had registered with them to use their address when they went to get an ID card, though they couldn't help you prove who you were to the DMV[i]. That was a very useful service, possibly the best help they could offer the homeless. It was also an efficient method of crowd control, because the first time you registered, they would scan your ID, if you had one, so they had records for everyone. They still insisted on taking your picture each time you registered at the shelter. That way, they had at least two pictures of every single person who ever slept there.

Helping you get an ID card was a good thing to do, in spite of its "Big Brother is watching you" shadow, because without one, you couldn't sell anything legally. The cops all knew the address of the shelter, and when they saw it on your ID, they understood that you were homeless. If you didn't have one when the police asked for it, so they could check your name and see if you had any outstanding warrants, they could grab you for "failure to identify."

> **Failure to identify:**
> Failure to identify occurs when an individual refuses to identify him or herself when a law enforcement officer stops them lawfully (by virtue of their being suspected of criminal behavior). Failure by the person so stopped to respond may constitute a criminal misdemeanor.

Everyone knew the front desk cooperated with the police, and that any information they had about you could get to them any time. A few swore they had seen pictures of "suspects" that they knew were taken at the shelter. Our friend only stayed there twice. He didn't sleep a wink either time because of the fifteen or so guys who snored. He'd stood in the line to register for the night a few times, used their shower, and then left. They checked you in, but they didn't check you out, so no one knew if you actually slept there or not.

It was much better to commandeer the bathroom in a restaurant for a while, listening for the sound of someone knocking on the door, as you wash as much of yourself as possible, as quickly as you could. Someone could knock on the door at any moment, and that gave you about two minutes to leave. It was always good to use soap, but you had to get your body soaped up, and then rinse it all off, and that means going over yourself twice. That takes longer, and you never knew if you'd have enough time. Restaurant managers don't like having homeless people around, and they don't like having their bathroom tied up. Ethnic restaurant owners were a little different. If they were Latino or Philippine, or Chinese, there was a good chance they might be understanding. Catholics are supposed to be nice to poor people. But you never knew.

Our friend knew a Mexican restaurant a few blocks away, outside his usual territory, which was constructed by converting a gas station into a restaurant. The toilets were around back, and the customers had to leave the building and go in the rear door to reach it. That meant it had more privacy than most places. He decided to take a chance. You needed to use the key to get in the men's room, and he couldn't ask for it unless he bought something. Once he'd asked for the bathroom key, they'd keep an eye on him, even if he was a customer. He could hope that it would be unlocked, or just wasn't completely closed. It was an old building, and the chances were good.

He had a razor that was probably good for one or two more shaves, but you can shave anywhere, and it wasn't worth staying in the bathroom long enough to scrape away his grizzled whiskers as he waited for someone to knock on the door. He could use the public bathrooms in the tourist market for that.

Instead of walking down the street and asking people for spare change, he decided to go behind the buildings and check the dumpsters as he went along. He needed a new T-shirt, and every dumpster seemed to have some cast-off clothing in it. You could see piles of dirty clothes in all sorts of odd places, and T-shirts were common. Any larger size was fine, but they were no good if they weren't big enough. If a T-shirt was too big, you could tuck it into your pants, but if it was too small, it left a band along the bottom of your stomach where the cold would get in.

It was easy to tell when a bag was filled with clothes. The plastic stretched across it in a certain way, and he could tell just by poking it. There was a bag of clothing in the dumpster, but it was all women's clothes, and no T-shirt. Women seemed to throw away a lot more clothes than men did. He kept going. The next one had a bag of bathroom trash, including a couple of used razors, but they didn't seem to be any better than the one he had now. He found a clean newspaper, and opened his backpack, took out his worn one, and threw it away, exchanging it for the new one.

Newspaper is a great insulator on cold nights. Sleeping *under* a blanket made of newspaper only works when there's no wind. You could line your sleeping bag with it, but he usually stepped behind a dumpster, dropped his pants, but not his long underwear, wrapped newspaper around his outer thighs between his pants and his 'skivvies', and left it at that. He could also put it under his coat, but then he'd wake up in the middle of the night sweating, faced with the choice of leaving the newspaper in place and getting even more overheated, or take it out, and enduring the blast of cold air.

The next dumpster stank too badly to be worth going through. It smelled like spaghetti sauce gone bad, and he didn't like spaghetti, even when it was fresh. It smelled strange, and gave him heartburn, but some people thought he was being arrogant if he turned it down when they offered it to him while he was panhandling. After this happened a few times, he started accepting it and putting it to one side. It happened most often when he was sitting with his sign ("The Greatest Nation in the World is Donation."). When another homeless person walked by, he would offer it to them. Sometimes he could bum a cigarette from them.

Another dumpster. Cardboard boxes. An empty milk jug. A bunch of electrical cords, all tangled together.

The case for a Beyoncé CD. He'd seen her name on magazine covers, billboards, and ads on the side of buses, but he had never knowingly heard a song of hers. Not once. He was pretty sure he'd heard her somewhere, from a boom box in the park, or in a shop of some kind, but he had no way of knowing *this* song was from *that* singer. In fact, he was almost completely cut off from all popular culture. It had been a long time since he had a home of his own with a sofa, a TV, and a DVD player, and he didn't spend much time thinking about music or movies, anyway.

The next dumpster had an unexpected surprise. A towel. It was a medium-sized one, and it had a rip along one side, as though a dog had chewed it up. He bunched it up and smelled it. It was fine. That meant he wouldn't have to use the paper towels in the bathroom to dry himself off. He wedged it between the bottom of his backpack and his sleeping bag.

The same dumpster also had a bag from Burger King. As he moved it aside, he could feel that it had some weight to it, so he looked inside. And there was a good amount of leftover food. There were French fries, but they'd gone cold and cold French fries are disgusting. There was also about two-thirds of a "whopper" hamburger. Dairy products gave him gas, but there probably wasn't much actual milk in the cheese, so he didn't bother to get rid of it. He ate it right there. He knew where it had been. It had been at Burger King, and then in a car. Someone took a few bites out of it and, for whatever reason, decided they didn't want to finish it. They put it back in the container, closed it, put it back in the bag, and then into the dumpster. If someone had eaten it in their kitchen, they would've put it in with all their other kitchen trash and it wouldn't have been in there on its own.

If anyone told him 'Don't eat that, you don't know where it's been,' he would've told them to use their common sense and ask; 'Well, where the fuck *could* it have been? The CIA doesn't poison hamburgers and then put them in dumpsters on the off chance that a homeless guy will eat it and die, taking his Chinese military secrets with him.'

Besides, nobody was watching, and no one would say anything about him eating out of the trash. In fact, he reflected, nobody cared what he ate, or what he didn't. He chuckled a little bit as the thought of a doctor asking; "Are you sure you're getting enough fiber?" flitted through his mind.

Today's dumpster diving was pretty good, all things considered. He remembered the Hello Kitty toys, and how he had gotten 20 bucks so quickly.

He kept walking, and opened the next dumpster he came to. The first thing that caught his attention was a fishing rod. He tried to think of a way to sell it, but didn't have any ideas. *Someone* would give him a few bucks for it. Our friend just didn't know who, or how he could find them. He'd seen fishing rods in pawnshops, but never bothered to look at the prices, so he had no way of knowing how much he could get for one. He looked closer and saw that one of the guides was missing. That's probably why it ended up in the trash. The only way to sell it was to collect a bunch of usable stuff and spread it out on the pavement as a sidewalk sale. But he didn't have enough stuff to do that, and putting it out on the sidewalk by itself and waiting for someone who wanted a fishing rod probably wouldn't pay off as well as sitting with the sign ("Homeless. Sick. Getting old. Please help"). He made a mental note to himself to find a place to hide things like that.

His last stash was in a strange little alcove at a construction site, behind some 55-gallon drums. Its plywood, which surrounded the site on three sides, was taken down a few days before, and all the stuff he'd hidden there disappeared. That was too bad. Sidewalk selling was always easy, unless the cops told you to pack it up and move on. There was a stretch of sidewalk in front of a fence, on one side of a parking lot. It was usually lined with people selling all kinds of things laid out on blankets, towels or cardboard. Together, they constituted a perpetual rummage sale, with constantly changing merchandise and sellers.

The people who lived in the neighborhood knew all about it and a lot of them looked at the goods whenever they went by. You could've made a living at it, except for the police. They were strangely arbitrary about telling the sellers (who were "Peddling without a license") to pack up and get out.

Peddling Without License:

"A peddler who sells or offers for sale or exposes for sale, at public or private sale any goods, wares, or merchandise without a county license, is guilty of a misdemeanor and shall be punished by imprisonment for not less than thirty days nor more than ninety days or by a fine of not less than fifty dollars nor more than two hundred dollars or both."

They would leave you alone for days at a time, and then one day, do a sweep and throw everybody out. They confiscated everyone's stuff a few times, but that meant they had to take it in to the police station, and they didn't like doing that very much. The trick to street selling was finding enough stuff that you could sell all at once. The more you had, the more you sold. One day's selling could need two or three days of dumpster diving, and a safe place to keep things until he had enough to justify spending a day selling instead of trash picking. The problem was hauling the stuff around. You had to find it, carry it to your cache, and then do it again, taking it to the sidewalk sale when it was time to sell it off. Then, you had to carry it back to wherever you are storing your things at the end of the day.

He looked into the next dumpster he came to and immediately closed the lid again. It was full of remodeling trash. Chunks of drywall, pieces of wood, and everything covered in a layer of plaster dust. Nothing there. Move on.

The one after that was a gift from the gods. It had a bag of clothing in it. He tore it open, and saw a pair of blue jeans, too small for him, and a green T-shirt, emblazoned with the words "Made with Real Yogurt." It was a lucky find. He needed a T-shirt, and there it was. He smelled it. Not too bad. It had a mild

Homeless: A Day in The Life.

odor of sweat and some kind of cologne. Masculine smells. A *lot* better than the one he had on, which reeked with the accumulated stink of his own sweat.

The same bag also had a pair of socks. They were the thin black kind and almost useless to him unless he put them on under his much thicker white ones. His socks were a mess, too; he'd have to change them when he got a chance. The gospel mission had them for free sometimes. The Salvation Army store was a better bet, and they were cheap. He jammed the socks into his backpack, right on the top. He'd think about them later. If they didn't work out, he could throw them away again. "Easy come, easy go."

Now that he had a T-shirt, it was time to make his approach to the bathroom at the back of the Mexican restaurant, called *Tenochitlan*, the Aztec name for Mexico City. He thought he might even have a good chance to find some Mexican food. They wrapped their burritos in aluminum foil, and if someone didn't finish theirs and threw it away, you could clean off the outside, pinch off the top, and what was left was clean and edible. Besides, burritos will keep for a while. In general, Chinese food went bad faster than Mexican, but you've still got to check each dish, one-by-one. You have to know these things.

On the other hand, looking for a burrito meant digging through restaurant garbage, the most offensive trash there was. Garbage bags with used diapers were usually closed up neatly. The smell was awful, but it wasn't that messy. Even baby poop, the most common form of human feces you found in the rubbish, was less horrible than most restaurant trash. With restaurant garbage, you take things only from the top layer, or not at all. Salsa sauce, with its chilies and onions, made Mexican restaurant garbage especially sharp and horrible. Still, half a burrito, weighing almost a pound, was a good find. He would see when he got there. He didn't want to be seen rooting through the garbage, and then be found taking over their men's room long enough to wash himself. No matter how charitable they were, they would still think he was a foul, dirty, offensive and otherwise pathetic human being. They'd warn their children to work hard so they wouldn't end up like him. He'd check the trash *after* he had washed, if he could get into the bathroom at all. "Timing is everything."

He got to the restaurant, approaching it from its back alley. The door was locked. He knocked lightly and got no response. It was empty, but he couldn't get in. He decided he would wait until someone used the bathroom, and when they left, he'd try to sneak in behind them. That meant he'd be there for a little while, but he was getting tired, and didn't mind sitting down for a while he waited.

He recalled that he had an unopened package of tobacco. He'd gotten involved in his work and just plain forgot he had it. He took it out, opened it, and extracted the thick rolling-papers. That was the great thing about Bugler. It came with its own papers. He rolled himself a cigarette, slowly packing in the tobacco, which was fresh and still a little moist. After a day or even less, it would start to dry out and crumble when he rolled a smoke. The first cigarette from a new pack was always the best, so he made it as well as he could, evening out the tobacco until it was uniformly thick. His fingers knew how much he needed. He didn't have to think about it. He pinched off the loose tobacco from the ends and carefully put it back into the package.

He remembered that his lighter was almost out of fuel, and hoped he'd be able to light up without struggling. The lighter ignited, with only a very small flame. It was just enough. He played his cigarette over its tiny fire, and puffed. It had been two or three hours since he'd had a smoke, and Bugler was strong stuff. A wave of relaxation came over him as he took his first drag on the cigarette, and he was shocked at how intense it was. This was one of those moments he lived for, but never really thought about. Tobacco was good. More is better than less.

It didn't matter that it was bad for his health. He knew that. Everybody did. But it was good for his mind. He sat there, puffing deeply, thinking he had enough to last him the rest of the day and into tomorrow, no matter how much he smoked. He watched the back of the restaurant, musing on its Aztec name, and congratulating himself on being cool enough to know what it means. Perhaps, one day, a situation would come up that desperately needed a white homeless man in his 50s to know what the word *Tenochtitlan* meant. He would be there, and he'd be the hero. Everyone would respect him.

Tenochtitlan. It meant "Under the prickly cactus."

The capital city of the Aztec Empire.

His hand rolled cigarette was burning low, and then he remembered that he still had almost a gram of marijuana from Tate, the perpetually optimistic Rastafarian in the park. He opened that up, broke off a pinch with his thumbnail, crushed it up, and then cursed himself for forgetting to take out the pipe first. He transferred the pot from his left hand to the palm of his right, losing a few precious scraps along the way. He got out the pipe, put a pinch of the Bugler on the bottom of the bowl, and then put the pinch of pot on top of it. Above that, another layer of tobacco, and then it was time to light it.

Once again, he confronted his failing lighter, which was running on fumes. He shook it vigorously, to get its few remaining drops of lighter fluid to evaporate, and hopefully give him one more flame. He put the pipe in his mouth and struck the lighter. He was able to light the pipe, but knew it would be a few seconds before he could do it again, so he puffed lightly to keep it burning while he held the smoke in his lungs. After a moment, he exhaled and immediately took the final hit. He had only put enough in the pipe for a couple of puffs anyway. As he inhaled, the ember grew, and his lungs filled with its smoke a second time in as many minutes. That was it. No more for now. He leaned back onto his backpack and relaxed. He saw that his cigarette had not gone out completely, and puffed on it to bring it back to life. He sank into a deep, peaceful place for a few seconds, and smiled. The tobacco rush on top of a good solid high was a nice combination.

Homeless: A Day in The Life.

He rolled another cigarette, not as well crafted as he usually made them, and lit it off the still glowing ember from the first one. If he took too long to roll it, the butt from the first one would have gone out and he couldn't have used it to light the second one, and he'd have take his chances with his nearly dead lighter once again. He wasn't going to do that if he had any other choice.

Now he was stoned and having a cigarette. It would have been the perfect moment for another coffee, but he was in position to wash at least part of his body. He could walk down a few doors and get one, but if someone used the bathroom while he was drinking it, he'd have to choose between spending more time waiting to get into the bathroom, or having his coffee cold. "You haven't got a microwave oven in your pocket, have you?" He'd wait.

He watched as an old Mexican man with a cane walked to the men's room and used the key from the front counter to let himself in. Old men can take a long time in the toilet, but that was no problem. It just meant he had to wait a little longer. Besides, he didn't want the man to finish too quickly, because that could mean throwing away his cigarette before he'd finished it. He puffed on it with a suspenseful intensity, trying to finish it at just the right time. It was getting short now, and wasn't worth thinking about, but he was stoned, so he thought about it anyway.

There was a noise from the bathroom and he got into

position to hold the door as the old man came out. The man was on a cane, so he wouldn't think that a homeless guy was trying to sneak in; he was more likely to assume that the next person was politely holding the door for him as he went through it with his cane. And that's exactly what happened.

As the old man opened the door, our friend pulled on it to open it a little further, and beckoned to the man to continue on his way out. He reached for the key, and the man handed it to him, not knowing he wasn't another customer. The clerk would probably think that the old man had just forgotten, and left it in the men's room, but they might not think about it at all until someone else needed it. Probably. He was overthinking it, but he didn't have anything else he needed to think about right then. Besides, it pays to plan things out.

Once he was in the bathroom, every second counted. Someone else could need it at any time. First, he pissed into the toilet; a more relaxing experience when you're not doing it behind a dumpster or in a corner of an alleyway, which put him at risk for the misdemeanor charge of indecent exposure. Then, he took off his coat, construction worker vest, shirt, and undershirt as quickly as he could. He dressed like a lumberjack. All his clothes were as thick as he could get them. The smelly undershirt was now garbage, stuffed into the bottom and covered over with used paper towels, so no one would notice that he'd been there. He turned on the water, adjusting it until it was as hot as he could stand it. Hot water. "God, that feels good."

He took a couple of the paper towels from the dispenser on the wall, soaked them in the water, and started washing himself, running the wet towels over every part of his upper body he could reach. Because he did his stomach first, it was the first part of his body to get cold, so he did it again. The second time around, he included his face, but without using any soap. He took a little liquid soap from the dispenser above the sink and rubbed it into his armpits, and then caught some of the warm water from the tap and splashed it there to rinse them out.

He grabbed a couple more paper towels, soaked them in hot water, and gave his armpits one more rinse. He was now officially "clean." Anything he could do from this point, before someone came looking for the key, was an extra bonus. He tried to decide whether to rinse his hair, or try to clean his groin. He put on the "new" T-shirt ("Made With Real Yogurt"), and noticed how good it felt compared to his old one.

If he got caught there, they might start keeping an eye open for him, so he couldn't wash there again later on. They could even put in a security camera. They were everywhere these days. The shirt and construction worker vest went on next. Now, it was time to take out the towel he'd found in the trash earlier. He wished he'd thought to tear it into two pieces before he got there. He'd have to make do by wetting one side of it to wash, and leaving the other side dry, so he could wipe himself off with it afterwards.

He dropped his pants, and pulled down his underwear, noticing that they weren't really in such bad shape. He'd worn much worse than what he had on now. Still, he wished he had an extra pair. He heard the voice of Mick Jagger in his head, singing, "You can't always get what you want."

He'd been there too long already, so soap was out of the question. He wiped himself down, front and back with the warm wet end of the towel. After squeezing out the water from the towel, he wet it once again, and wiped himself a second time. He dried himself off, noticing that there seemed to be more gray pubic hairs there than the last time he looked. It didn't matter. He wished it did, but it didn't.

Clean and dry now, he pulled up his pants again, underwear first, and then his long underwear, and finally his pants, and there still hadn't been anyone knocking on the door. He decided to take another chance and rinse his hair. Running the water on the edge between warm and hot, he lowered his head into the sink. The sensation of warm water rolling over his scalp was exquisite, and he allowed himself a few seconds of debauchery, just feeling his head getting warm, without doing anything else.

He stood there, doubled over with his head in the sink. He scratched his scalp, trying to dislodge as much dirt as he could, squeezing his hair, and enjoying the sensation, even as he tried to stop any water from getting on the floor. Really, it was impossible to avoid. The best he could do was to spill as little of it as possible. After a moment, he shut off the water and ran his hands through his hair to squeeze out as much as he could. He picked up the towel, found the dry side and dropped it over the back of his neck. He rubbed his head, not because he wanted his hair dry, but because he didn't want any water running into his clothes. He combed his hair with his fingernails.

He was done. He dropped his towel on the floor, and used his foot to wipe the water he'd spilled. Then he dried the counter around the sink and rolled up the towel. He put on his coat, wishing it wasn't quite so dirty, but knowing it would be hard to get another one as warm as the one he had. Next, he got his backpack on, deciding that he would think about trying the thin black socks later. He urinated again, just because it was easy and convenient to do it there.

He felt a subtle wave of regret pass through him as he left the bathroom. It was warm in there, there was hot water, and the toilet was friendlier than a brick wall behind a dumpster. He didn't flush the toilet. That would tell the cashier that someone was in the men's room. They might notice that the old man with the cane hadn't returned the key, and figure out that someone was in the bathroom who wasn't supposed to be there. "Restrooms are for customers only."

He liked to think that he was a responsible and ethical beggar, so he took the key with him as he left the bathroom, and walked into the restaurant. He went to the counter and asked the cashier, as he handed over the key, "is this yours?" The clerk smiled and said

"Yes. Thank you." He quickly took a piece of peppermint, wrapped in plastic, from a little bowl in front of the cash register. The clerk would think he had earned it by handing in the key, and would offer no objection. He didn't particularly like peppermint, but he could take one for free. The little candies by the register are *supposed* to be free, and that made it all right to take one. The clerk probably noticed that he was homeless, but if they suspected anything and went to check the men's room, they wouldn't find any mess, and their supply of paper towels wouldn't have diminished noticeably. They also wouldn't see his stinky cast off T-shirt, buried under layers of used paper towels.

It was a success. He was clean, sort of; top and bottom, front and back. He had even managed to clean his hair, but only with hot water. Any visit to a private restroom to wash your hair with shampoo was a dedicated operation. He wouldn't try to do anything else in the same visit. The instructions said "Lather. Rinse. Repeat.", but he never repeated. Not once, ever.

He threw the towel into *Tenochtitlan's* trash, scanning the top for a half eaten burrito, but the dumpster received the towel without offering any viable food in return. That was okay. He didn't actually have a contract or any kind of deal with the dumpster. It hadn't broken any promises. Like most homeless people, he was superstitious (he would never pick up a penny if it was tails up), and felt it was bad luck to get angry at the trash.

After leaving the restaurant, he headed around to the back door once again, this time to throw out his towel in the dumpster. It had been used to clean the ass of a homeless man, and even he wouldn't consider holding onto it to use again later. He had no illusions about his hygiene.

Todd Murphy

CHAPTER THREE

He rolled himself another smoke, to celebrate the victory he found in cleaning his body without anyone noticing. That was three of them in less than forty-five minutes. Bugler papers are short, so their cigarettes don't last long. He'd have to slow down a little, to make his tobacco last. He decided to head back to 'his' park, not because he had something to do there, but because he couldn't think of anything else to do. There was still time to take his sign ("Homeless Vet. Please help.") to the financial district and sit in the street, to see if he could collect a few more bucks.

He wished he had a good book to read while he sat there, but taking the time to visit a thrift store to find one was probably not a good idea yet. He was likely to get lost in the sensation of being an ordinary shopper in a heated store, busy deciding what to buy. It was very rare for him to go into a store to buy anything without knowing exactly what he was going to get and exactly how much it cost. Thrift stores were the cheapest, but you had to take time to look at the merchandise, look over the books, and think about what clothes you wanted. He could get absorbed in those places and stay there for hours, but he'd feel crestfallen when he left and had to face the realities of the street once again. He almost felt normal in a thrift store. So far, the day had been pretty good, and he didn't want to tempt himself into a depression.

He'd seen enough of the inside of dumpsters for a while, even though he always felt content while he was doing it. He could take whatever he wanted, and no one would call it stealing. He could spend as much time as he wanted going through each one, and nobody would tell him to hurry up. It was fun, too. Anything could turn up at any time.

Once, about a year earlier, he had actually found a gold bracelet, marked "14K" - fourteen carat gold. The clasp was broken beyond repair, and whoever owned it probably didn't realize it was gold. They may have just thrown it away when the clasp broke. Because he had an ID, he could take it to a gold trader he knew about in the financial district in a building dedicated to the wholesale jewelry trade. Nobody cared who you were or what you looked like if you had gold in your pocket. The only thing that mattered there was how much gold you had. He walked into the building, with his backpack, bedroll, dirty clothes, and near-certain stink. When the guard at the door asked him where he was going, he said, "The gold dealer on the fifth floor." To underscore his point, he held up the bracelet, and said, "I'm here to sell."

The guard just waved him on in. He took the elevator up, got off, and rang the bell to be admitted into the office, where he found a special plexiglass cage he had to stand in. Once inside, he had to put the gold in a box that slid back and forth between the cage and the office. The dealer on the other side of the screen weighed it, and told him that, because the clasp was useless, he could only buy it by weight. It had no value as jewelry. That was fine. He already knew the clasp was broken, so he didn't mind that they weren't going to pay him a jewelry price. He just wanted to make sure he wasn't cheated for the value of the gold, just because he was homeless. The old man asked him if he had ID, which he did. The clerk pointed at a sign that showed exactly how much they were paying (by the gram or by the pennyweight) for gold that day. That was why he came to this place, whose name he could never remember. The amount they paid when they bought gold was posted on the inside of the barrier, so it was the same for everyone. If you had ID, you got the price listed on the wall. If you didn't, they wouldn't give you a penny. Gold dealers operate under strict licensing and regulations. They can buy from the homeless with ID, but not from a billionaire without one.

There weren't many situations where the homeless got equal treatment, but this was one of them. The money he got for the bracelet put him in a hotel room for two nights, as well as buying him an "eighth" (1/8 of an ounce) of pot, cigarettes, and a few restaurant meals, including a McDonald's big Mac combo meal, and curried chicken with rice (to go) from a Chinese restaurant. He still thought about that curried chicken from time to time, even though it'd been more than a year. The first night in the hotel room was wonderful; chain-smoking cigarettes, taking hit after hit of marijuana, crop-full with *hot* French fries, rice and chicken. As he watched HBO, he reflected on the message in his fortune cookie, which said, "Your destiny will reveal itself soon." It also advised him that eight was his lucky number.

He brushed his teeth a dozen times in those two days, and spent six hours altogether soaking in the bathtub, reading the *Lord of the Rings* for the 10th time. He went to a laundromat and washed his clothes, wearing a hotel bathrobe.

He pulled himself out of his reverie, wishing he had someone he could teach how anyone can sell gold. He was a master of the homeless arts, but never had an apprentice.

Without really thinking about where he should go, he started walking back towards his home base, the park where he slept at night. This time, he walked down a different alley, also surrounded by apartment buildings. He'd look in the dumpsters again, even though he was getting tired of it. Whenever he went anywhere, he was confronted with the same choice; he could either walk down the street and ask people for spare change, which usually didn't pay off very well, or he could dig things out of the trash, but then he'd also have to *sell* whatever he found, so that extracting wealth from the garbage was a two-phase process, while panhandling was a yes or no, now or never occupation. Either people gave money, or they didn't. If they did, they did it *now*.

Overall, he preferred the dumpsters and there was never any harm in looking in a few more. When he walked through the alley on the next block, he found that they'd been emptied that same morning. So, as he made his way towards the park, he moved down one block, and went through another alley. This one had office buildings on one side, and apartment buildings on the other.

These were mostly empty, too.

Rather than move the opposite direction for two blocks, to get out of the area covered by that morning's trash collection, he decided he would just head straight towards the park. The dumpsters were open 24 hours a day, and he was getting tired. Besides, his feet were starting to hurt. Time for a break.

He walked into the park and found his friend Nick sitting on his usual bench. Nick was one of the few people he knew on the street who could have an intelligent conversation. He used a few drugs, but wasn't deeply addicted to any of them. Nick kept away from needles, and didn't drink alcohol.

"Hey, Nick."

"How's it going?"

"Well, I'm alive. Still alive. What you doing, man?"

"Not much. Just walking around, seeing what I can find."

"You make any money?"

"Some. I found a whole bag full of Hello Kitty toys. Brand-new. I got 20 bucks for them from this Chinese guy with a kid who was wearing a Hello Kitty shirt. That kid was real happy about it.

I got some tobacco. You want to roll one?"

"No, man. I'm good. I got some cigarettes."

"Can you watch my bag while I go get a nickel from Tate?"

"Of course. You put it right there. I won't let anyone touch it."

Anybody else would've asked if our friend was going to share some of that nickel bag with them, but Nick and he were friends and knew, without asking, that he was going to get him stoned.

Nick was 75 years old, from the Horn of Africa. He fought in two guerrilla wars, and then came to America, where he volunteered to go to Vietnam to help him earn his citizenship. Like most black men, and also like most immigrants soldiers, he was assigned to combat duty. That was three wars altogether, and more than enough for anyone. One was plenty for our friend. Nick didn't like to talk about it, but not because he had PTSD (he probably did), but because the armies he fought with eventually won their wars. Their Marxist-Leninist leadership turned corrupt and degenerated into a kind of mafia. He was very disappointed about that.

Homeless: A Day in The Life.

The inspired leadership of the glorious workers and peasants national liberation movement, men trusted by Chairman Mao Ze Dong (the loving friend of all children), left aside their essays on proletarian internationalism, and instead focused on bills of lading for AK-47s, 7.62mm ammunition, hand grenades, and good shoes. It was an "armed struggle", and the arms were worth a lot of money.

Nick was too old to start another life's work, and his health was terrible. So he spent his days wandering the streets, looking for tourists. He would approach them and ask, in his Tigrinya accent, if they wanted to hear a real African story. A lot of people said yes. He would tell them a story, usually something traditional from his country, and sometimes stories he made up himself. He was a good storyteller, and people paid him in cash, straight to his hand, where his Social Security caseworker wouldn't see it, and so they couldn't report it. They'd cut his benefits if they knew. However, even though Nick's habits weren't very expensive, about half of the money he got this way went for drugs; mostly pills, pot or crack. He never made a lot of money, partly because nobody ever wanted to pay much for a story, and also because once he made enough, he'd head straight back to the park, and buy something to get high on.

Nick was the only person he would trust to watch his bag. The man would never let him down, and he would do whatever he could to help him. Nick had gotten off the streets through a city program to provide housing for homeless senior citizens. When Nick signed on for the program, he was 70. He was

73 when they got him a room. So Nick was homeless, even though he had a home. It might be better to say that, even though he had a room, with its own small kitchen and a bathroom, he still thought and acted about the same as he did when he lived on the streets.

There really isn't any point in trying to reform yourself when you're 75 years old and your loved ones have dismissed you as a hopeless drug addict and there's also no way to make yourself useful to the world. Nick accepted himself as he was, because the only alternatives were too fanciful to dwell on. "You can take the man out of the street, but you can't take the street out of the man."

He sat next to Nick's place on the bench and broke up some of his pot. They didn't share a pipe; they each had their own. This was handy - when they could arrange it. If the police see two people smoking together, passing a pipe back and forth, they'll understand that they can make two arrests in the same action. One person smoking pot in the street seemed to bother them a lot less than two. So, nobody ever saw Nick and him passing the pipe between them, and not many people saw them smoking in the first place. The ones who did, didn't pay much attention. They took turns taking their hits for the same reason. It was another point where the police were a little weird. One cop would see someone smoking and instantly want to make an arrest for public intoxication. Another one would walk by and just tell you to put that away. You never knew. Best to be careful all the time.

Public intoxication:
Public intoxication, often called being "drunk and disorderly," is a legal charge alleging that a person is visibly drunk or under the influence of drugs in public.

"You hear any news, man?" It was one of Nick's ways of starting a conversation. He was very interested in politics, but didn't keep up on the news. Politics had been a great disappointment to him.

"Aw, man, you're not gonna believe this, but Trump decided to recognize Jerusalem as the capital of Israel (he learned that this morning, looking at the front page of a newspaper in a vending machine).

"That motherfucker. He's crazy. He don't know what the Palestinians and the Arabs will do about that. He hate terrorism, but he do like that and they gonna be bombs blowing up all over the Middle East, and nobody gonna ask, "Why they do that?"

"I know. It'll piss off anybody who doesn't support Israel. Could be the first step towards war."

"No, man. Any little thing goes wrong over there, and everybody think it gonna be war. But it never happen. They never gonna start a war over there. People afraid that everybody's going to go crazy at once, and they all scared to be the first one."

"Maybe so."

"You know how much money American government people make in Israel and Arab countries by almost-going-to-war? They make millions. Billions. All the people the government pay to *stop* war over there - they all gonna be unemployed if a real war starts. They gonna be replaced by generals, and when they come home, they gonna work for a lot less money. Americans in Israel and these Arab countries work for the government for ten, twenty, thirty, years and that's all they know how to do. They know how to pay bribes. They know who to kill. If somebody *really* try to start a war, they kill him. True story."

One of the interesting things about Nick was that he believed in conspiracy theories, but without anybody actually conspiring. The political, economic, and military influences were enough to control events. All you had to do was understand them, and you could profit from any nation or group of people. They manipulated themselves, by doing what comes naturally; chasing money. He thought there was a conspiracy to keep Israel and the Arab countries *almost* at each other's throats, but without ever crossing the line into a real war. Real politics happened behind closed doors and most of the time, had nothing to do with the news. The media was controlled by the ultra rich, military interests, the deep state, and demonic groups who practice black magic. Nothing was trustworthy. Nick was a Marxist who had given up Marxism, because it's theories didn't work, but he hadn't found a replacement.

The guy was intelligent, and well worth talking to.

Nick was smoking some of the pot our friend had given him, out of his own pipe, when another homeless guy approached and asked for a hit. Our friend had seen this guy before, and didn't like him very much, so he put his pipe, with its faded marijuana leaf design, back in his pocket. He'd wait until the interloper had gone away. He wasn't stingy about his pot, but the guy was kind of obnoxious, and he wasn't going to do anything that would encourage him to hang around.

Nick's response was blunt; he handed his pipe to the guy, telling him to take one hit and then beat it. "You get out of here. I'm talking to my friend now. I see you later, Man."

Nick spoke excellent English when he wanted, but he could also drop the fine points of grammar, and talk like he'd never lived anywhere but the streets.

"Nick. I'm gonna get some coffee from the little store down that way." It was a filthy convenience store, with a coffee urn in the front, styrofoam cups, sugar packets and little plastic containers of half-and-half. They had the minimum arrangement for selling hot coffee, and their price reflected it. The cup of coffee that would cost over two dollars at Starbuck's, or a dollar sixty at 7-Eleven, cost $1.25 at the little store.

It was run by a Korean family, who said as little as possible to anyone who came in. They seemed to hate the rich tourists just as much as the homeless. But then, interacting with a couple of hundred people a day, none of whom know anything about the city they're visiting, and who act like they're your best friend because they buy a pack of chewing gum, can be tiresome. They didn't play any music in their shop, which together with its grime and poor lighting, made it a little eerie. They watched the homeless people carefully, but our friend knew what he was going to buy before he set foot in the store, and took care to leave as soon as he was finished there. He got his coffee, some potato chips, an apple, and a chocolate bar. Just enough to fill his stomach, and made his way back to where Nick was sitting. He sat down again, and offered the cup to Nick, who took a sip, and handed it back.

Nick wasn't a coffee addict. He was marginally addicted to several drugs, including crack, but coffee wasn't his "thing."

They had run out of energy for talking about politics, and just sat there for a while. Soon one of the park's "crazy ladies" started screaming.

"You get the fuck away from me. You don't touch me; you don't talk to me; you don' even *look* at me. I will fuck you up. You don't touch my shit. Ever."

She went off on someone regularly, and nothing could calm her down. She wasn't *completely* crazy - she only screamed at people if they bothered her, though it didn't take much to set her off. Once she started, it took a few minutes before she would quiet down, even if the cops showed up.

"I ain't doing nothin'. I be mindin' my own business,

and this motherfucker started grabbing on my shit. I'm just gettin' him away from me."

The cops would stand around her for a few minutes, trying to talk her down and get her to stop screaming. They had taken her in a few times ("disorderly conduct"), letting her pack up her things because they knew if they tried to separate her from her "gear," she'd just start yelling again. All too often, when they arrested a homeless person, they would leave their possessions on the ground, to be scavenged by anyone who wanted to. Even if they released you without a charge, you could still be left with everything-you-owned-in-the-world taken from you. The medicines you needed could be in that bag. You could say you had pictures of your family; sanitary napkins. No matter what you told them, if they wouldn't let you pack up, the result would be the same. Whatever it was, you lost it. Failing to stay out of their way carried a heavy penalty.

No one in his position could avoid the cops completely, but he kept clear of them whenever possible. If he saw a group of police on one side of the street, he would cross it and walk on the other. They would hassle our friend once in a while, not because they thought he'd broken any law but because they knew his face, and they liked to keep tabs on the "regulars" on their beat. They knew he wasn't one of the dangerous ones, but they kept an eye on him all the same.

So far, he hadn't been arrested. It wasn't luck. He lived within the law as much as he could. He didn't shoplift, carry weapons, touch hard drugs, make scenes in public, or challenge the cops. He didn't even drink except late at night, when the alcohol would help to keep him warm. Alcohol felt weird to him, and hangovers hit him very hard. He didn't get into fights. Once in a while, someone would just walk up to him and demand that he hand over his tobacco, money, or something else. He either gave in, or pled that he didn't have any. Once, someone even came up to him, and demanded that he give them all the money he panhandled everyday. He just said no, and as he walked away, the would-be extortionist called out, "I'll be watching you," in a malevolent tone of voice. He knew someone *that* aggressive wouldn't last long in the park. He'd get busted in just a few days, and that would be the end of him for a while. In fact, our friend never saw him again.

Nick said, "Roll me one of your cigarettes, man." So, he rolled one for Nick, even though he knew Nick had some cigarettes in his pocket. Sometimes you just feel like a change of pace, and he knew Nick would give him a cigarette if he asked for one. Having two types of tobacco was a luxury. Nick was happy to oblige when he asked for one of his Marlboros a few minutes later. He took two more pinches from his small supply of marijuana, and put one in his pipe, and the other in Nick's. They scanned the space around them, and seeing there were no cops, they lit up. He used Nick's lighter, because his own was so low on fuel. He made another mental note to himself to pick and check any lighters he saw on the ground. It was surprising how often they turned out to be good.

"Man, that woman going to get herself tossed in jail, sooner or later."

"Yep. One of these days, the cops are gonna have to do the paperwork, and put her in the nuthouse. She's trouble. I just leave her alone."

"Yeah, that's the best thing to do with her."

Nick agreed. The best strategy was to avoid all trouble, ignore any insults, and just keep going.

The meek shall inherit the earth.

He was feeling good. He'd eaten. He was stoned. He had a cigarette, and a cup of coffee. It was still warm. He sat there, basking in the company of his only friend, a "real" friend. But Nick was 75 years old, had three kinds of cancer, and had been through two heart attacks. He wouldn't be around much longer.

He knew the answer already, but he still asked, "So how's your health?"

"It's bad, same always. The doctors tell me to quit smoking crack, cut out the cigarettes, and no more coffee, too. I told them 'Fuck you, Man.' I'm gonna do what I want."

"You ain't gonna quit anything for your health, are you?"

"I take my medicine, but I'm not gonna give up

anything so I can live longer. Nothing. I like to smoke, and I don't give a fuck what they say. Listen to me: the hospitals are evil; like hyenas. The hospital don't care anything about how you feel. They just want you to live longer, 'cause the longer you live, the more you get sick, and then somebody gotta pay the bill. It's all for the money. They don't give a fuck about anything else. They know what's going to happen to me, and they write it down. They say I'm gonna die from cancer or another heart attack, and that's what's gonna happen. Then the doctor gonna look at the paper and he say 'I was right.'"

"Yeah. Doctors love to be right."

"Yeah, man. Lawyers, too."

Nick continued, "You know what happen to me. I go to see one doctor, and he say I got prostate cancer, and he want me to have the surgery. I say, 'no fuckin' way.' You know what that doctor did? He took me to court."

He had heard the story a half dozen times already, but that was okay. It was an amazing piece of modern stupidity, and it gave him an opportunity to count his blessings. He didn't have cancer.

"Yeah, you told me. Un-fuckin'-believable. How can they do that?"

Nick continued, "So, I have to get a lawyer. A free lawyer. What do they call? *Pro bono*? So I have to go to some office, tell them I have no money, but a doctor was suing me to have the surgery. You know how long it took them to take my case? Less than one minute. They look at the papers they give me, and it say right there, 'petition for court order requiring surgery'. They never heard of anything like it, so they give me a lawyer, some kid, and he say to me 'we can't lose.' This case is too crazy. The judge won't believe it."

"So we go to court, and the lawyer give the papers to the judge. The judge read the papers, and look at the doctor and say 'are you crazy? You can't sue a patient to force them to accept your treatment. Do you know what the word 'ethics' means? I'm asking you a question. Before I throw you and your case out of my court, I am ordering you to stand up and tell me why you filed this suit."

As our friend understood the story, the lawyer stood up and said, 'My client needed proof that the defendant had refused the treatment, because without it, the defendant could sue my client for malpractice. His state of poverty makes him a litigation risk.' They might not be suing Nick *exactly* because he was poor, but they never would have sued anyone who was rich in the same circumstance. Motherfuckers.

Nick continued, "The judge put his head in his hands, and you could hear him breathe, like he try not to laugh. He tell that doctor, 'Never do this again. The courts aren't here to protect you from malpractice. Get out of my court room, and you better hope I never see you again, because if you ever come in here for a *good* reason, I'm going to remember you're one stupid doctor. I don't think your lawyer's very smart, either."

Our friend smiled as he heard the story. He loved the punch line "one stupid doctor." He stayed away from doctors as much as he could. They could be more dangerous than the police, and even more frightening. You go in with a runny nose, and you come out with a diagnosis of pancreatic cancer, and you're gonna die a painful death. Maybe they put you on a program, and then you get to be homeless while going in for chemotherapy once a week. Medicines were okay. Tylenol was a sublime blessing. Taking their pills was no problem, but the minute they say, "We want to run some tests," or tell you that you need surgery, you lose all control over your life, and his life was already beyond control.

Nick was right. Your life's purpose and how much you could enjoy it was more important than how long it lasted. Revolutionaries just can't accept a meaningless life. Our friend had been homeless long enough to know his chances for ever living like a normal person were practically zero, and no doctor, no matter how well-intentioned, could make his life any better. At best, they could keep it from becoming worse. Besides, he was homeless, and that meant that they wouldn't give him anything for pain except aspirin or Tylenol, so he walked on his sore feet, drank lots of water or took Rolaids for heartburn, and rested for hours at a time, next to his sign ("Seeking human kindness"). His stomach was a mess, though he didn't know exactly what was wrong. Living on the streets was very stressful, and our friend had been doing it for years, so he suspected it was an ulcer, just like the ones rich executives have, though he got food poisoning more often than they did.

He knew he had to be careful what he ate. Dairy products, spicy food and soy were more trouble than they were worth, unless he was very hungry. His solution was simple. Keep looking in the trash cans, and pass on anything he couldn't eat. The tourist areas had good edible trash; the tourists and yuppies often put out their leftovers in "doggie bags" or take-out containers where anyone could find them. He had eaten some good meals that way, and never needed to go hungry for long. He thought it was ironic that the one thing he could find the most easily, food, was also the one thing that people were most willing to give him. Homeless people sometimes die in the streets, but not from starvation.

"I won't give you any money, but I'll buy you something to eat."

"Okay. That's fine, but I can't eat dairy, soy, or chili."

Some people would argue that beggars can't be choosers, but he would just shrug for an answer. If it makes you sick, don't eat it.

Sometimes they would go into a store, and come out with some food; sometimes not. It didn't matter. Food was easy. Tobacco, coffee, pot, a dry sleeping bag, and shoes were the real challenges.

He remembered the socks he took out of a dumpster

earlier. Taking off his shoes and socks, he put on the thin black ones, then his foul-smelling normal thicker socks over them, and then put on his shoes again. He stood up to see how they felt, but they didn't seem to make any difference. He kept them on anyway. Changing them again would be more trouble than they were worth. Besides, he was with his friend, and didn't want to pay too much attention to his feet.

"Man, it's starting to get cold at night. I wish I had a tent." A sign saying, "Can you spare a tent?" wasn't going to do any good. He'd have to scrape the money together and then check the thrift stores to see if he could find one. At fifteen or twenty dollars, it was a major investment. Fortunately, the St. Vincent De Paul thrift store usually had them. Tents were big, and easy to see. The main risk with them was that the cops would appear, tell you to close it up, and "move along."

That was very close to throwing people out of their homes, and generated a lot of protest, noise, and more than a few arrests. More often, they would tell you that you're not supposed to be here, and then walk away ("Just a warning this time"). After a few days, if they saw you were still there, they might take the tent away or just cut it up. If you yelled at them, you got busted, and the police would have to do the paperwork while you sat in a cell, and whatever was in your tent would be scavenged out of existence.

The police patrolled the tent encampments to keep them quiet as much as to protect the people that slept there. They were more tolerant when the weather was colder, and he calculated that he should think about it again in a few weeks. Homeless encampments with tents were great places to sleep, but the panhandling was terrible, because nobody had any money, and the neighbors were crazy. Anyone could wake you up for any reason, at any time, and there was no one to complain to. "Tent cities" didn't have any place to put your trash. There was no water, no showers and no toilets, but you had to *go* somewhere. If you weren't careful, you could get busted for shitting in the street, "creating a nuisance" and committing "indecent exposure."

Besides that, your neighbors, in their tents, might yell at you about the smell, even though they knew there wasn't anywhere else to go. Get a piece of newspaper. Get behind a dumpster, some bushes, or a large cardboard box in an alley. Shit on the newspaper, fold it up, and drop it in the trash. If somebody sees you, that's their problem. Even the cops avoided hassling people while they were shitting, and preferred to stand by and wait until you were done before giving you a ticket or putting you under arrest. They didn't like that either. If the case got to court, they'd have to tell the judge that they arrested someone while they were taking a crap, and that made them sound ridiculous during the hearing, no matter how skillfully they used the sterile language of legal procedure. Some problems were more trouble than they were worth.

The tourist market men's rooms were open to the public, including homeless people. It was another blessing, but the market locked them at 7 PM, and opened them again at 9 AM. Scores of homeless people used them every day, but as though by some miracle, they were never very dirty. Not that he would mind, but if a men's room is filthy, and there's a homeless guy in it, someone will always assume that they're the one who made the mess and complain about it.

His mind wandered a lot when he was stoned. Nick interrupted his thoughts.

"So what you gonna do, man?"

"I don't know. I might go sit with my sign ("Recovering stock broker. Please help."), or maybe I'll go dumpster diving again. I'm on a roll today. No, I should sit with the sign first, and check the dumpsters tonight."

He groaned a little as he stood up and groaned again as he maneuvered his arms into the straps of his backpack. They weren't really sore. He just grunted a lot.

"Okay, Dog. I'll check you later."

"Okay, man."

"I'll be back this way."

They "dapped" their knuckles together, and our friend turned to leave.

He walked through the tourist market. Noticing a

lighter in the street, he picked it up and tested it. No good. A half-full cup of coffee sitting on a trash bin caught his eye, but he decided he'd had enough coffee for now. It was time to piss. He went into one of the public toilets, and after using the urinal, glanced in the mirror. "Shit, I'm getting old." He looked older than his actual years. The stress of living on the street had taken its toll on his body, both inside and out. He decided it was time to shave, as a gesture of rebellion against his accelerated decay. "Resistance is futile."

He fished his razor out of his bag, and turned on the water. Hot water always felt good. He wondered how it was that the bathrooms had hot and cold water, letting anyone use as much as they wanted. Whatever.

He first splashed his face with hot water, and then took a paper towel, soaked it, and pressed it against his whiskers. The heat felt good. Someone came in, and went straight into a toilet stall, breaking his solitude. He was no longer alone. He was acutely aware of the difference between what it felt like to be alone, and how he felt when there were people nearby. There seemed to be a change in the very air he breathed when he knew there were other people around. He set his mind to "rig for silent running." The less attention he drew, the less chance that anyone would make trouble for him. After soaking the paper towel again, and holding it briefly to his face, he started shaving.

He hadn't shaved in a few days, and the stubble was getting rough. Still, he worked his way through it, wishing he had a fresh razor. The one he had was almost played out. In fact, this had to be the last shave with it. He knew he wouldn't cut himself, but it was going to take longer. He didn't like standing in front of the sink, shaving his face, while a perfect stranger, neat and clean, washed their hands in the one next to his. "So how about them Giants?"

There was almost nothing he could talk about with ordinary people. It really did seem like he was an alien, visiting Earth, and trying desperately to fit in by never offending the earthlings. Of course, he *couldn't* fit in, but that was something he avoided thinking about. It was the reality of his life, and even though he still let it shape his instincts, he still pushed it out of his conscious thoughts. "That way lies madness."

Eventually, the man came out of the toilet stall, and stopped to wash his hands. Our friend watched him out of the corner of his eye, ready to move out of the way so he could reach the paper towels, which were inconveniently placed on the wall, instead of between the sinks. The man washed his hands, and reached for a paper towel. Our friend got out of the way quickly, making it easy for the man to grab one. He dried his hands in no time, and got out of the public bathroom with the scruffy looking homeless guy in it.

Our friend didn't like interacting with the public, and they didn't want anything to do with him. It was an arrangement that worked. He was an untouchable; a pariah. He knew it, and he tried not let his shadow fall on a yuppie's food, lest it be polluted. 'Thou shalt eat no owl, nor defileth one's hearth with the offal of even a clean beast.'

Homeless: A Day in The Life.

The shaving was coming along nicely; he was almost done. Another man came into the bathroom, used the urinal, and left again without washing his hands, all in less than a minute. He looked like he was in a hurry.

He finished shaving and threw the razor away. If he didn't have it, he wouldn't be tempted to try to shave with it again. As it was, his cheeks felt a little raw. He blotted his face with warm water once more, mostly because he could, and because it felt good. He splashed some water on them to force the whiskers down the drain. He rinsed out his mouth, and he was done.

He looked in the mirror and told himself that he looked a little younger and healthier with his stubble gone. He did, too.

Todd Murphy

CHAPTER FOUR

Now it was time to head back to his spot in the financial district, and sit down with his sign ("Just trying to get by. Please help.") He wished he had a long and engrossing book to read, but stopping by one of the thrift stores would slow him down and take him too far out of his way. He'd find a newspaper to read.

He turned a corner and found himself confronted by about eight cops and three police cars. Usually, he would've backed away, or pretended that he was going to cross the street, away from them, but he had already made the turn, and there was no way he could get away from them without drawing attention to himself. The best thing to do was to keep on going as though he didn't see the cops. He always noticed them, and they saw him noticing them. Taking stock of the situation, he saw that there were three homeless guys sitting on the ground, their backs against the wall. The police were gathered at the outside of the sidewalk, and one of them was watching our friend as he walked along.

Then the worst thing happened. One of the police stepped in his path and said, "Can I talk to you for a minute?" A shaft of cold fear sliced through his torso.

Our friend answered the only way he could:

"Yeah. Sure."

"You know any of these guys?" That was probably their main question.

"No, Sir."

You always had to call the police "Sir." It made it clear from the beginning that you weren't angry with them and that you intended to be respectful. Respect meant subordination and compliance, which they referred to as "cooperation." It was one of the unwritten rules. You don't have to respect the cops, but you always had to act like you do. He remembered one of Nick's jokes: "The homeless are only ever guilty of one crime: contempt of cop."

"I have ID. Would you like to see it?"

It was always better to offer to let them look at your ID than it was to wait for them to ask. Otherwise, they could try to get you talking and say something that could incriminate you. Usually, they asked to see your ID only after they talked to you, when they had you sort of "figured out." If you *offered* to show them your ID, it circumvented their usual procedure. They had to avoid saying that they *didn't* want to see it, so they never refused.

"Yes, please."

The cop said "please." That was a good sign. It

seemed to say that he didn't expect our friend to be a criminal, or turn violent, or have a psychiatric episode right there.

Our friend told the cop, "it's in the inside pocket of my jacket". First, you tell the cop where your ID is, and only then reach for it. Putting your hand in your jacket unexpectedly can make them worry that you're reaching for a gun, and the way they reacted to *that* could ruin your whole day.

He took out his ID and handed it over. The policeman looked at it and scrutinized his face. Check. It's the same person. The cop walked away and got into one of their cars. He worked on the laptop there, looking him up to see if he had any outstanding warrants. Our friend wasn't worried about it. Several weeks had gone by since he'd even talked to a cop, and he knew they weren't going to find anything on him. All the same, the few minutes between the time when you give your ID to a cop and when he returns it to you can stretch out into an eternity. Stars can be born and collapse into black holes in the time it takes for a cop to check you for outstanding warrants.

His life would change drastically without his ID. He had heard a couple of stories about how police had refused to return an ID to its owner, but he was pretty sure that these were either urban legends, or tales from a rare "monster cop" on an especially bad day. The story always ended the same. The unfortunate street person then had no ID, and was accosted by another cop soon after that, who demanded he show his identification. The victim would say they didn't have one and blame the police for taking it from him. The cop would arrest him for "failure to identify," and then bring him to the police station, where they found something else to charge him with. He doubted it was true. In his experience, the police stuck to their procedures, and would rather invent a completely fake charge than break one of the rules while making an arrest for a real one. But then, you never knew.

The seconds ticked by while he waited for the cop to give him back his ID and let him go on his way. The other cops, busy with their three suspects, paid no attention to him. He spotted a lighter on the ground, picked it up and struck it. It worked. It's flame was a lot stronger than the one from his dying lighter. He wouldn't have found it if the police hadn't stopped him. So, the cop checking his papers had done him a little bit of good. Because of this, he didn't have to spend $1.49, plus tax, to buy another lighter. For a moment, his mind glided over what the lighter would cost *with* the sales tax, but balked at figuring out what 8.5% of $1.49 would be. He didn't like doing math in his head, and his math skills failed him completely as he sweated out the short, but still interminable confiscation of his ID. Besides, it doesn't matter how much you don't spend. It only matters how much you do.

The policeman got out of the car with a gentle expression on his face, which told our friend that everything was fine. The cop stopped briefly to talk to one of the others. Neither of them betrayed, even by a glance at him or the three suspects, what they were talking about, and he wondered if there was something out of the ordinary on the computer. He knew he shouldn't ask. In fact, he should say as little as possible.

The cop handed him back his ID, and said, "You can go."

"Thank you, officer."

"You stay out of trouble, now. Hear?"

"Yes, Sir. Thank you."

You always had to thank them. It helped them to think you were either scared of them, or honestly respectful, and that you "are not the droids they're looking for."

The cop asked: "By the way, are you a veteran?"

"Yes, sir."

The cop pointed to himself and said "Iraq."

Our friend pointed to his chest and replied "Lebanon." Some people could tell, just by looking at you.

He put his ID away, picked up his backpack, and started down the street, cursing himself for failing to avoid the cops, while congratulating himself for not smelling enough like marijuana to get the cop's attention, and even cutting short the policeman's routine by offering to show his ID.

He decided to go a block further than usual to sit down with his sign, to make sure he was completely hidden from them. Sitting right on the concrete was uncomfortable and cold, so he picked up a cardboard box standing next to a trashcan and flattened it down to make a mat for himself.

His favorite spot was too close to the cops right now, and he didn't want them watching him. They might be tempted to make another arrest, and the fact that he had just been checked was no guarantee that another cop in the same group wouldn't do it again. So, he had to re-think his strategy, and once again decide where the best place to sit was. He sat down on some steps that led up to a fountain in front of an office building. It was actually on private property, not the sidewalk, and that meant two things. One, the police couldn't ask him to leave, unless there was a *no trespassing* sign or a complaint, and two, he could get busted for it if he didn't leave immediately when asked. Really, you were told, not "asked".

Trespassing
"Trespassing is defined as the act of knowingly entering another person's property without permission. Such action is held to infringe upon a property owner's legal right to enjoy the benefits of ownership."

But trespassing wasn't a big concern. Most of the time, all you had to do was move on when the cops told you to. The main thing was to pick a spot where there was a lot of foot traffic, but not too crowded for him to be seen. The steps in front of the fountain were perfect. He'd used that spot before, and never had any trouble there, but he still thought it through again.

He sat there with his sign, watching people walk back and forth. About half of them, engrossed in their cell phones, didn't notice him at all. No one stops to think of these things, but when cell phones became a major addiction, people were less able to notice bums sitting on the ground, and this cut into the amount they could collect in their begging bowls. They just scrolled past them. No one puts change in a bowl they can't see.

Still, people glanced at him, and it wasn't long before someone dropped 31¢ into his bowl. One quarter, one nickel, and one penny. His sign read, "Will work for job opportunity." It was one of his better brainstorms. When he used that one, it was a little like just being unemployed, and nobody said, "You can get a job. Why aren't you working?" He always answered the question, saying, "If you're so sure, then *you* hire me."

The truth was that nearly all homeless people, those without a roof over their heads, were unemployable. Nobody would give them a job. You can show up to a job interview with a backpack, but if it has a bed roll attached to it, then your chances of getting hired shrink down to invisibility. If two people apply for a job, and one of them doesn't have an address to put on the application, they'll hire the one that does. No one will hire you without a telephone number and an address, and you need references, too. A job application form separates the homeless from the rest of the population just as surely as the bill of sale once separated southern plantation owners from their slaves.

A mother with two children walked by. One of the kids, clearly too young to read, stopped to look at him, and his sign. The mother said, in a harsh whisper, "You stay away from that man," and the kid skibbled back to rejoin its mother. "What's he doing, mommy?" "I'll tell you later. Just stay away from him."

That always stung. Every time. Once in a while, he could forget that he was an outcast, but when something like this happened, he was forced to remember the state he was in and the circumstances he lived with. He was a beggar. A nobody; lower than a snake's belt buckle. His thoughts continued this way for quite a while, his own worthlessness crashing to the surface, no matter what he did to push it away. He wished he had a book. He got up and walked to the nearest trashcan, hoping for a newspaper to distract himself. He found one of the local advertising newspapers. Not as good as an actual newspaper, but it was something. He looked through the classified ads on the back page. They offered legal help for drunk drivers, quick divorces, a horse show, and an Asian massage parlor that promised a sensual and relaxing experience. None of it had anything to do with him. With his self-esteem still reeling from being labeled the dirty man that small children shouldn't talk to, the classified ads weren't enough to lift his spirits.

A woman with a silly expression came up, and in a contrived fruity voice said, "I'll pray for you. God will help you. You'll see." So far, God hadn't been very helpful, though overall, the day wasn't going so badly.

"If you want to, ma'am."

This happened to him pretty often. People offered kind words, or smiled at him, thinking that a smile can brighten up someone's day. He never saw it that way. The person who offered a smile instead of a coin or two was just being a compassionate cheapskate. He didn't mind so much when people didn't give him money; he knew that only a small percent of the people walking by were going to give him anything, but it rankled when people offered him things that he couldn't use. He never complained when it happened. People like that meant well, and he knew they were often strapped for money, too. If he gave them a rude response, they might answer in kind, and that could turn into a shouting match, and nobody put any money in his bowl when there was an argument going on. It was important to keep things quiet and relaxed.

Years earlier, while he still lived at home with his wife and kid, he'd seen a homeless guy in his neighborhood, who the locals called "Torgo." Torgo was the worst beggar in the history of the world. He was fat, and he wore T-shirts that were too small for him, exposing his lower stomach. Torgo hated pennies. If someone gave him a handful of change, he would throw the pennies on the ground, and yell things like "Don't you know the coffee shops won't take pennies?" Or, "Give me some rolls to put them in." From time to time, ordinary people, thinking, "beggars can't be choosers," would give him nothing but pennies. This would send him into a rage, and he would call after them, yelling, "douchehead," or "fuckwad," after them as he threw their pennies into the gutter. If someone walked by smoking a cigarette, he wouldn't ask them if they could spare one. Instead, he would *demand* they give him one immediately, "Give me a fuckin' cigarette. Don't you know you're not the only one who needs a smoke? What the fuck is the matter with you?" Eventually, a local newspaper ran an article about him. Apparently, he represented a new low among the homeless.

Something was wrong with Torgo. Most likely, the stress of living on the streets, and the effort it took to beg a dollar or a smoke got the better of him, and he just started acting as rude as he wanted to. You only saw him in that neighborhood at night, where he would wait for a certain coffee shop to put its leftover pastries, usually bagels, in a plastic bag, and set them on top of a trash bin for the homeless to take and Torgo waited for that moment. The coffee shop would close at 8 PM, and the leftovers would come out about twenty minutes later. Sometimes they were late, and of course, Torgo would get angry. Our friend stopped to talk to him a few times, always giving him a dollar, because otherwise it would waste his time. He told Torgo he shouldn't get angry at the coffee shop employees, or they might stop putting out their leftovers (which actually violated the health code regulations), and then there wouldn't be any for anyone. Our friend took a few Danish pastries out of that bag himself, even though he wasn't homeless then. He did it because he could, and the pastries weren't bad at all. He didn't know it at the time, but it was his first taste of food from the street.

Now that he was homeless himself, he reflected on Torgo's frankly impossible way of panhandling, and thought that maybe, just maybe, telling people to go to hell might actually work. He might try it one day, though it didn't really fit with his personality, and he had no chance of winning the fight it would create, sooner or later. It might work on a street where there were lots of bars, at night, so that a good number of people in the street would be drunk, but that also made actual violence more likely, and the first rule he lived by was to avoid trouble as much as possible. Torgo's technique would just have to wait.

He let go of remembering Torgo, and brought his mind back to the present. Sitting with his sign and a begging bowl worked a little better when he made eye contact with the people walking by. Of course, almost half of them had their faces in their cell phones, so it wasn't easy. He tried anyway because there wasn't anything else to do. Again, he wished he had something to read. He didn't make as much money when he was reading, but it was a lot easier. The only interruptions were when someone actually gave him money, and he would look up to thank them.

Occasionally, he would see someone who he thought

might be a good "mark." He'd try to catch their eye by waving at them, and then ask, "Can you spare a little something today?" Usually, they just kept going, but they dug into their pockets just often enough to make it worthwhile.

Strangely, the people who looked depressed were most likely to respond to this approach. Maybe they thought God would reward them. Overall, poor folks were more likely to give than rich ones. Rich people could be charitable, but they were a little calculating about it. They donated to charities (registered as nonprofit organizations) for the tax break, but that was very different from giving a couple of bucks to a homeless man on the street. Once in a while, when he caught an obviously rich man's eye, he would say, "You ever been as poor as me?" Sometimes that would get them to pull out a dollar, but just as often, they would reply that they'd never let themselves get that poor (or words to that effect), simultaneously refusing to give him anything, giving themselves a superheroes' immunity to poverty, and implying that people were homeless because they "let themselves" become poor. People are more willing to believe the myth of "rags to riches" than the truth that riches can turn into rags.

In fact, he thought to himself, just sitting here and looking forlorn was probably about as effective as calling out to people. Whatever.

The people who bothered him most were the ones he thought of as "power of positive thinking" people. They'd say things to him like "be optimistic," or tell him to let go of his "poverty consciousness." Their way of seeing things was as far from his perspective as you could get. Happy thoughts didn't make good things happen. At least, not for him.

He knew what *negative* thinking could do to him and did his best to avoid it. Fear, depression and anxiety were his mortal enemies. There wasn't much he could do to avoid being afraid. His life was full of things that would scare anyone. But getting depressed was different. It could take him days get over it. Even talking to his friend Nick couldn't pull him out. The only thing that would lift him out of a depression was a stroke of luck. The elation that came over him when he made a really good trash find, or someone gave him a few dollars all at once was enough, but you couldn't count on that happening very often.

He mused over his fortunes. Most homeless people believed in luck. Sometimes, for a few days in a row, it seemed like he could do no wrong. Every other dumpster yielded something worthwhile. Asking for spare change, he would come up with a "donation" every few minutes. At other times, also for days at a stretch, it would seem he could do nothing right. The bowl would stay empty, except for the two or three coins he put in himself, as "seed money." The dumpsters would yield nothing. Fortunately, no matter how bad his luck was otherwise, the trash bins on the street always gave him something to eat, though it was harder on Sundays. Then, he would have to check the barrels in the tourist street, over and over again. Because it was a tourist area, and people were from out of town, "exploring" the market, there was a lot of ethnic food and sometimes even the remains of luxury snacks in the trash, so the eating was good. Sundays were busy days in the market, and new leftovers could appear at any time. If he walked through the market, checking the garbage, and nothing turned up, he could just turn around and do the same thing again on the other side of the street; over and over until he got what he needed. It's not rocket science.

The food supply in the trash cans never seemed to fail him, but there were a lot of homeless in the area, and the competition could be fierce. He'd seen more than a few arguments break out over the remains of a bagel and cream cheese, or half of a chocolate chip cookie. These brief clashes almost never turned into serious fights, and most of the homeless people, even when they were really hungry, respected the two unwritten rules that governed that kind of trash picking. One, "first-come, first-served," and two, "only one person to a trashcan at a time." If someone was going through a garbage bin when he came to it, he would wait until they were finished. Most of the time they got the good stuff, and the best thing to do was just carry on and look somewhere else. You might even end up with better food than the other guy did. There were lots of rubbish bins in the tourist market, so it was easy to just keep searching until something turned up. A lot of trash pickers were only interested in bottles and cans. They were specialists, who usually didn't make their money any other way. In general, they were taciturn and irritable. With each can bringing in only five cents, they had to work long, hard hours.

Bottle and can collectors have territories, and they'd get angry if they found someone else going through the trash in their turf. If that happened to him while he was looking for food, he would just hand them a bottle or can from the barrel (if there was one), and tell them he wasn't looking for cans. These guys always worked with big garbage bags, and if you didn't have one, their rules shouldn't apply to you.

Today's luck had been good, and that was the first sign that tomorrow's luck would be too. Good and bad luck seemed to run in phases, with each phase being two to four days long.

He remembered his tobacco.

Another one of his superstitions was that it was a good idea to be seen rolling a cigarette in the street, because that way, people understood that he really was poor; too poor to afford a pack of cigarettes. He rolled it very slowly, so that passersby could see that he was sincere, or at least, that's how he imagined it. He recalled that he had found another lighter, one with some life left in it, and was pleased about that again for a few seconds. He lit up, and took a deep drag. Tobacco was his friend. The Lady Nicotine might be an unhealthy love, but his feelings for her were sincere. He longed for her presence whenever she was absent, and scrounging for cigarette butts was a chivalric quest that honored his lady fair.

Strangely, in spite of his heavy smoking, and moderate dependence on marijuana, his lungs were fine. He could breathe to his full capacity, and for a while, after trash picking an oximeter, a little medical tool that slips on the end of your finger, and tells you how much oxygen is in your blood, he measured his own oxygen level, and found that it always read 98 or 99. The batteries for the device soon ran out, but not before setting his mind at rest about his lungs. He wondered if sleeping outdoors helped him because it gave him more fresh air than most people. If he was short of breath, it was because of his stomach and the gas that appeared after he ate. Probably, it was something to do with the ulcer he thought he had. If he had any other health problems, he didn't want to know about them. Today's worries were enough for today. Jesus said something like that, and added, "Let the morrow take care of itself." He had no trouble with that part. He usually didn't think about tomorrow enough even to decide not to worry about it, except when he was going to sleep, and mentally inventorying his cash, his tobacco, and his marijuana supply.

Clink. A quarter. Rattle. A small handful of change. "God bless you, sir." A few minutes passed. A dollar bill. It was like that. Nobody would give him anything for half an hour, and then suddenly there would be several people in a row. He thought that when people were walking behind someone who gave him money, it inspired them to do the same. When they saw others ignoring him, they ignored him too. They were sheep. Or maybe a wave of magical Chi passed through the air, making everybody generous for a minute or two.

Homeless: A Day in The Life.

He made a mental note for his book on the psychology of homelessness he was never going to write. Maybe the problem was that none of them, living in their warm homes, however cheap, knew how to respond to a person living in absolute poverty. When you're warm, you don't think about what it's like to be cold. By the time they had made up their minds that they should give him something, they'd already walked by. The same could be said for their decision not to give him anything. They *didn't* decide. Not giving him money was a default behavior; an automatic position. So was the uncomfortable way they ignored him. They just didn't know what else to do.

When they noticed someone giving him money, they thought to themselves, "That's what I should do." When they saw someone look away from him, they would do the same, as though the random stranger just in front of them had a more reliable moral compass than they did. Homelessness was not something you learned about in Sunday school, college, or high school. Nobody taught anyone anything about it. Nothing. So, they just didn't know. "Forgive them Lord, for they know not that they're ignorant as fuck."

He took the dollar out of his bowl so that people walking by wouldn't think he had enough money. Some people. If they see you with one dollar, they think you have a million. He put the dollar in his pocket and leaned back, scanning the people walking past. "Spare some change?"

"Here you go, buddy." A man in overalls, wearing a tool belt, handed him a five-dollar bill. "I don't care if you use it to get drunk. Good luck." The fellow had a roughened face, and our friend wondered if the man had been homeless himself. Maybe not. Workingmen were always more generous than people with real money, a thought that reminded him of something that always made him angry. Once, sitting close to where he was now, a rich man, whose gold watch and three-piece suit displayed his wealth, walked up to him and said, "I didn't get rich by giving money away," and then walked on. He didn't give a shit how the man got rich. Smug bastard.

But someone just gave him five dollars, and that was good panhandling. He thought about packing up and moving on now that he'd made a few bucks, but realized that there wasn't anything in particular he wanted to buy just then. So he decided to just sit there and relax. His feet always hurt, and that put some pressure on him to stay where he was for a while longer.

His good luck continued. More change. A couple more dollar bills. He thought he might like to get up and go to a thrift store, and see if he could find that good book to read, but decided that he would do that later on, if he did it all. He made a lot of plans that he didn't follow up on. He was accountable to nobody but himself when he changed his mind. That was one good thing about living on the streets. No one was entitled to demand an explanation from him for anything, except the police, and they only wanted to know if he had any outstanding warrants, not if he was being responsible, following through with his plans, and brushing his teeth.

The foot traffic kept going past him, and he thought about packing up just long enough to duck into an alley, crouch behind a dumpster, and take another hit of his pot. He would do that, but not just yet. He still felt pleasantly high from his last hit, and he knew if he smoked too often, it would stop feeling good, and would only make him feel stupid and tired.

Another small handful of change fell into his bowl from an unseen hand. "Thank you. I appreciate it." He didn't even look to see who had given it to him though that was kind of rude. They answered "No problem," and he looked up to see a woman, probably in her 50s, with a careworn face. She walked on. Her clothes showed her as neither rich nor poor.

He'd seen other panhandlers, sitting with their signs, listening to music on their iPods, and wished he could do the same. He'd found a few in the trash and on the street over the years, but always sold them right away. As long as he had an ID, he could keep on selling things like that to pawnshops, and get a good price for them. Someone had told him to always delete the music, so they wouldn't think he stole it. But that didn't matter if you had ID. If it was stolen, then he and not the pawnshop, was responsible. If it wasn't stolen, then nobody would ask anything about it, anyway. He hadn't spent a lot of time with portable music players, so he couldn't always figure out how to delete the songs. It didn't matter that much. Garbage isn't stolen property.

He never had a music player for himself. Besides, if he spent more than a few minutes listening to music, he'd feel a little beaten down when he stopped. The sounds coming into his ears could fill his mind, and the empty, blank feeling that came over him when he took the headphones off was depressing. There were a couple of stores downtown that played opera or classical music through their sidewalk speakers, as though that would keep homeless people from congregating there. It didn't work in his case. He liked classical music, and once sat in front of one of these stores, very late at night, and listened to Beethoven's sixth symphony, almost the whole thing. No one bothered him, and it was about forty-five minutes of tranquility. When it was over, he didn't even feel depressed. He could hear passages from it running through his head for a couple of days afterwards. He'd heard it many times before, and remembered almost all of it. The pizzicato counterpoint in the fourth movement was audible ambrosia.

No doubt about it. He was bored, but futility, insignificance and monotony were occupational hazards of panhandling. His ass was getting uncomfortable from sitting on it too long, so he stood up, rubbed his buttocks, tucked and pulled at his clothing, scanned for police (you don't always see them when you sit on the sidewalk), and sat down again.

Panhandling itself wasn't against the law, but nearly anything you did *while* panhandling could be an infraction, like *soliciting*, or *obstructing the sidewalk*.

Soliciting:
Solicitation refers to any unlawful request or appeal, either oral or written, or any endeavor to obtain, seek or plead for funds, property, financial assistance or other thing of value, including the promise or grant of any money or property of any kind or value.

Obstructing the sidewalk:
A misdemeanor wherein a person, having no legal privilege to do so, recklessly interferes with passage on a public thoroughfare by creating an unreasonable inconvenience or hazard.

Asking people for money (without being aggressive) was actually legal. Nevertheless, our friend still liked to know when the police were around.

Begging:
The State Supreme Court, focusing on the fact that sidewalks are traditional public forums where the First Amendment prohibits the government from imposing restrictions based on the content of someone's speech, found two sections of a City "begging" ordinance to be unconstitutional content-based restrictions on free speech.

The people kept walking by. He smiled and nodded at a couple of other street people he knew from the park, and they smiled and nodded back. It wasn't time for conversation. A police car drove by. The cops paid no attention to him. An elderly woman with a dog walked by, and the dog stopped to smell him. The old woman jerked on its leash, and said to our friend "I'm sorry. He just does that. He doesn't mean any harm." Our friend replied, "No problem." The old woman, struggling with her dog, never thought to put any money in his bowl, but he never resented very old people for not giving him anything. Sometimes, except for the roof over their heads, they weren't any better off than he was.

Another dollar bill. "Thank you. I appreciate it."

Suddenly, he felt the need to use the toilet. Time to take a shit. That meant going back to the tourist market, about eight blocks away. His feet hurt, and he knew he couldn't walk very quickly. He had no choice but to pack up and go. He'd made about $13 in an hour and a half. Pretty low wages for doing security guard detail over a bowl of coins, but he wasn't worried about that. $13 was enough for any one of several things. Another meal, real cigarettes, or a trip to the thrift store to find more padded socks, and hopefully the good book that had been persistently nagging him the whole day.

He returned the bowl to his backpack, put it on, and folded up his sign. Now, to walk eight blocks to the toilet. There were other places closer than that, but that was the nearest one where no one could try to stop him. "Restrooms are for customers only."

There were two in the market, and he always chose the one farthest from the center. It offered a better chance for some privacy. This time it was full, except for one stall. He felt a rumbling sensation on the left side of his stomach as he sat down, and that meant diarrhea. He was going to do the "Hershey squirt," and there was nothing he could do about it. If he worked hard at it, he might think of something more humiliating than becoming that horrible obnoxious man in the next stall who shits making loud spattering noises, farts and stinks up the place. His sense of shame from this kind of performance around other people was vastly out of proportion to his actual offense. He found himself thinking, "Kill me now, Lord. Take me home."

Someone in the bathroom said, "Jesus! What's that smell?" Of course, the man knew exactly what that smell was. They were in a room with a bunch of toilets, and they never smell like incense. Nevertheless, our friend hung his head a little further, dreading the next eruption, and imagining that the other people in the room would like to take him out and lynch him. His mood was so desolate that he'd probably let them. As it happened, the men at the urinals were soon gone, leaving only one other man in the room, in the stall next to him. He shouldn't have let it bother him, but he still felt horrible about stinking up the place.

In the same way, he dreaded farting in front of people. It was bad enough being the dirty, stinking, ugly, old, cantankerous, and uncouth barbarian that people warn their children to stay away from. When he farted he imagined that, in that exact moment, he became doubly disgusting to everyone around him. The leprosy gnawing at his dignity and self-regard advanced with each public fart.

A sharp pain, about three inches below his navel, told him that more was coming, and he braced himself. He wondered what he had eaten and decided it was probably some Chinese food he found in a dumpster behind an office building the day before. It looked good, and it smelled fine, but it had shrimp in it, and it could have sat unrefrigerated by someone's desk overnight. Food from office building trash was usually pretty good. It was taken out every evening, and was mostly leftovers from someone's lunch, bought on the same day. The shrimp was probably just too old. He knew better than to eat any seafood from the trash, but it was good, and he was hungry. Now, he would pay the price in pain and semi-public humiliation. The event he expected passed, along with its matter, and the pain stopped just as quickly. Even though he was still using the toilet, he flushed it the instant the flow had stopped. That would cut the smell. The man in the next stall gave a sharp outbreath, "whew!", but said nothing. He tried to remember that they wanted to stay away from him as much as he wanted to stay away from them.

He heard the guy in the next stall flush, and put on his belt. He washed his hands. Our friend heard the sound of paper towels being pulled from the dispenser, and then being used to dry them. The man left. He was alone again. Thank God. Now, he could grunt and strain as much as he wanted, and there was no one there to think he was an uncultured beast; dirty inside and out. He didn't believe he could read their minds, but he couldn't imagine they could think anything else. He knew *disgusting* when he saw it.

After two or three more spasms, flushing the toilet each time, he knew he was finished, and went to wash up. He would often skip washing his hands unless he'd gotten something on them, but this time he felt so grossed out at himself that he wanted to wash them well, almost as a ritual of religious purification. And the hot water felt good. "No more two day old shrimp."

Todd Murphy

CHAPTER FIVE

He decided it was time to do something different. He *would* go to the Salvation Army store, and check his bag behind the counter (a rare luxury). Then he'd wander around, looking for books and new socks. He could take the load off his back for a little while and get warmed up. But the Salvation Army store was twelve blocks away. It was too far to walk, so he'd have to take the bus, but that usually wasn't a problem. The bus fare was $2.50, but the drivers were flexible about it. Many of them would just wave the homeless into the bus, and hand them a transfer, and let it go at that. Some drivers would let you stand at the front and tell your story, but most didn't want to hear it. They weren't in denial the way most people were, ignoring him whenever they could; they knew the homeless people didn't have any money. They also knew that the bus fare, paid in cash, really was a little too high. A bus pass, good for a month, cost about seventy bucks, so it was easier for our friend to just pay the fare one ride at a time (unless he could get on for free) than to try to come up with that kind of money all at once.

The bus stop was only a block away, and as he walked there, he remembered that bus stops were a kind of safe zone. When you're sitting at a bus stop, nobody, including the police, wondered what you were up to. They knew: "He's waiting for the bus." It's not loitering.

He rolled another cigarette and looked down the street to see if the bus was coming. If it arrived while he was smoking, he would either have to throw it away, save the butt, or wait for the next bus. He could see that there was no bus coming in the next couple of minutes, so he lit it up and stepped away from the bus stop. "No smoking within 25 feet of the bus stop. City ordinance, 102.23/gofuckyourself.54"

He stood there and smoked his cigarette while keeping an eye open for the bus to appear down the street, and enjoying the sensation of not having anything to do. Most of the time, he pushed himself to stay busy constantly, doing whatever he could to make even a little money. He was busy even when he was just walking down the sidewalk, looking for anything he could see on the ground. He picked up coins, cigarette butts, lighters (which he checked, and usually threw back into the street), pens, and anything else that looked like it could be useful. He also kicked any cigarette packages he saw. He could tell whether there were any cigarettes left in the pack just by the sound. It was surprising how often there were, but you had to check a lot of them to find the one that still had a smoke or two in it. It only took a second.

You don't ask people for change when you're waiting for the bus. You don't set up your sign because there isn't enough time for it to add up to anything. You can go through the trash, but garbage cans at bus stops don't yield much besides the half-eaten snack foods people throw away before they get on. "No food or drink allowed on metropolitan buses." He didn't want anyone to see him take food out of the garbage and start eating it on the spot. It grossed them out. It was okay to take food from the trash where people could see you, but you had to put it in your pockets, and eat it somewhere else. You don't want the people who see you take food from the trash to see you eat it. And you don't want the people who see you eating to know your food came from the trash. The thoughts of ordinary people became supernatural weapons when they were disgusted with him, and they attacked his self-esteem irresistibly. He left the trash alone.

There wasn't anything for him to do while waiting for the bus. Standing there and doing nothing felt good. His cigarette smoked down, and the bus approached as he finished it. Perfect timing.

The bus stopped, and the doors opened. Our friend waited until everyone else got on, and only then approached the driver. He didn't want to hold up the line with his story.

"Hey, man. I'm sorry, but I don't have the …"

The driver knew what he was going to say before he said it and just handed him a transfer, waving him onto the bus. One of the good drivers. The bus carried pictures of the "driver of the month." It always talked about how friendly, punctual and dedicated they were, but the only real criteria for our friend was how well the driver could see when someone was broke, and not be a prick about letting them ride. This guy was his driver of the month. A good man.

He could *pay* the fare, but that didn't mean he could *afford* it.

He wasn't broke, but $2.50 to get to a store where he would spend about that much made it bad economics, and cutting the fare out of the equation made it cost-effective in terms of money, foot pain, energy consumption (he was almost always tired), and overall strain. There were times he felt like he was a draw horse, hauling himself around as his own cargo. This strange reasoning seemed to justify his efforts to avoid the bus fare. He didn't think about it very much, or very deeply, because he actually believed it was wrong. Poverty should be its own excuse, but it wasn't.

He walked through the bus. His backpack, with a sleeping bag rolled up and lashed to the bottom, advertised his status. Another homeless guy. Making his way through the bus, looking for a place to sit down, he saw everyone sitting next to an empty seat turn to look out the window or bury themselves deeper in their cell phones. No one wanted to look directly at him. He got to the back of the bus where other homeless passengers tended to congregate, and took a seat next to an old black man who looked as though he was homeless, too. ("How y'all doing?" "Gettin' by. Gettin' by.") He could feel it when he sat next to someone who found him repulsive. It was better to sit alongside someone who looked like they would understand. His radar could always pick them out

Once again, he had a little time with nothing to do but sit and relax. After a few minutes, the bus stopped about a block from the Salvation Army store, and he got off from the back door, so he wouldn't have to walk past the driver again. He checked his pocket to be sure his bus transfer was still there, because he could use it to go back downtown. Glancing at it, he noticed that, although the policy was that transfers were only good for ninety minutes, his was cut off so that it was good for three hours. When he headed back to his territory, he wouldn't have to tell his story to the bus driver. He could just flash the transfer and get on. "Easy, peasy, japanesy."

He went into the Salvation Army store and waited at the cash register to check in his bag. They had a rule in their store that said you had to leave your bag, backpack, or purse at the front counter. They didn't intend it this way, but it meant that they would hold our friend's bag, and even take responsibility for it while he was in the shop. He handed it over, and was given a card with a number. "Sorry, but it's heavy." "That's okay."

His whole body felt lighter without the backpack. He enjoyed the sense of freedom and it helped him feel like he wasn't that much different from the other people in the store.

"Can I have the key to the bathroom?"

The old lady at the counter handed it to him, and pointed to a corner in the back of the store. It was attached to a huge kitchen spoon, making it impossible to lose.

The Salvation Army store had a toilet, and they would let anyone use it. He had to collect the key from the front desk and then go where the old woman had pointed. The bathroom had a door that locked and only one person could use it at a time. Privacy. Sweet solitude, if only for a few minutes. He sat down, and more of the bad shrimp with sweet-and-sour sauce was soon liberated. The pain just below his naval came and went. After using the toilet, he stopped to wash up. As usual, it was more to enjoy the hot water than to satisfy his sense of hygiene. This time he focused on his ears and the back of his neck. He pulled a paper towel out of the dispenser, soaked it in hot water, wrung it out, also wiping as much of his back as he could reach and then did it again with a dry paper towel. That was enough for a thrift store men's room. The place was crowded, and someone else would need to use it soon. He couldn't stay there very long; their cheap goods were too important to him for him to take a chance on getting thrown out of the place ("… and never come back again"). When he handed the key back, the old lady smiled a little, and he saw she had no idea he'd been washing up in the washroom.

He walked over to a bin with some thick sports socks and took out a pair. Plain white, like he always wore. That was easy. They were ninety-nine cents, as he knew they would be. They were new, but that came as no surprise, because most thrift stores don't handle used socks or underwear.

He made his way over to the book section, and scanned the shelves, looking only for thick books in the standard small size for novels. He could fit one like that into his coat pocket or one of the pouches on the outside of his backpack. It limited his reading, but he would only allow himself to buy books in that one size. If the book was larger than that, then he had to store it in the main compartment of his bag, and that was harder to get to. It would slow him down if the cops told him to move along while he was reading.

Looking over the cookbooks, history titles, the volumes on pet care, and the inspirational self-help books, he felt annoyed at how many of them were useless to him. He saw one on Chinese astrology and thought to himself that he must have been born in the year of the cockroach. There was a book he didn't need. All he needed was a novel to occupy his mind while he was sitting with his sign. He thought about making one that had an arrow pointing into the bowl that said, "Click Here to Unsubscribe."

He found a copy of "The Pillars of the Earth," which was easily over 500 pages. He'd read it before. When he read books again, it didn't matter if his mind got foggy, or he skipped over a paragraph. He already knew the story, so it didn't matter. He wasn't looking to learn anything, or to admire the author's style. All he wanted was a book that would stave off his boredom. All paperback books were one dollar, so a long novel was a better deal than a short one.

Knowing it would probably be the last warm place he'd be that day, he took his book over to the furniture department, and sat down in a big comfortable chair. He started to read, and the author's artistry began its work. Immersed in its words, he started to forget that his feet hurt, and that his life was probably ruined beyond repair. He forgot about the bad shrimp. He forgot he was homeless.

Smoking pot helped keep his mind together, but reading was the best way to really forget his troubles. As he thought about this, a nasty fragment of his personality spoke up and said, "There's nothing in your life *but* troubles." That was true, but eventually, a good book would even shut up his internal cynic.

He sat there reading for perhaps half an hour before he realized that he'd been there long enough, and they might think he was just loitering in their store. So he got up and walked around some more. He looked over the books again, to see if there was a better choice, but there wasn't.

It was a good thrift store, and its merchandise reflected nearly every aspect of life in America. The shoes for children were decorated with pictures of cartoon characters. The clothing on the mannequins was mostly for women, and the body types were always svelte and sexy. This is America. Be young and beautiful. You're supposed to be having fun.

He went over to the computer section, the only place where he might consider spending real money, because he hoped to have a laptop once again, when the higher powers decided it was time. But no laptop. The store now sold them on eBay, shipping them out by mail, and they didn't have them on the shelves very often. Nevermind. "Not meant to be right now."

He found a pair of sunglasses with big peace signs over the lenses, in psychedelic frames. fifty cents. He decided to buy them. It might be a good way to get a little more attention when he was sitting with his bowl. Maybe a sign that said: "Peace." It could work.

For a moment, he considered looking at the shoes, but the ones he had on now were in pretty good shape, and he could cut the pains in his feet by getting a pair of footpads. Cheaper that way.

He walked through the sporting goods section. No tent.

He'd been in the store for almost an hour, and soon the staff would start wondering when he would leave. It was getting boring. He walked by some shelves covered with children's toys, noticed a Hello Kitty popcorn maker, and remembered his success in the garbage earlier that day. It was time to leave, and his next thing should be to do a little more dumpster diving, unless his feet began to hurt too much.

When anyone else went to the Salvation Army, and checked in their bag, they were always relieved to get it back, but he always felt a twinge of regret. It would return to his back, where it belonged, and its normal ten and or twelve pounds would become a part of his body weight once again. He handed in the tag they gave him when he went into the store. The older Asian woman who retrieved his bag looked a little annoyed, not only at how heavy it was, but the sleeping bag attached to it also made it harder to lift above the counter. He knew she could tell that he was homeless, and she was a nice old lady, so he apologized, saying, "Sorry to give you more work to do." She smiled and said she was happy to do it. Her accent revealed that she was probably from the Philippines.

After paying for his stuff, he took his book and jammed it into one of the pouches on the outside of his backpack, remembering that it really was a good novel, and that he might even be able to start reading it again as soon as he'd finished it. He also remembered that it was long enough that he was bound to feel disheartened when he was done with it. Books were like good friends, and when you came to the end, your friend had died, and you briefly mourned their passing. He was already thinking of the book as though it was almost a living thing, but that didn't prevent him from forcing it mercilessly into his pack. It was kind of like having a good friend you treated like shit.

He left the store and stepped into the street, feeling the strong difference between the warmth of the store and the cool air of the street. He thought it would probably be cold tonight. No big deal. He had newspaper in his backpack, to wrap around his legs under his pants, and his sleeping bag was dry. So were his shoes. His woolen knit cap was thick enough that it didn't matter how cold it got. He had to have one. He was in his 50s, and his hair was getting thin. At one time, so long ago that he never stopped to be grateful for it because he didn't need its insulation back then, his hair was so thick that he couldn't wear a hat, even in the coldest weather. His scalp would get all sweaty and start to itch. Now, keeping his head warm was a matter of survival.

He started walking, and realized that the dumpsters in this neighborhood would have almost nothing but trash from apartments, and that was good. He'd move through the alleys, searching for what he could find as he went, just seeing what turned up. "Business as usual. Same old shit."

Even though he only had to walk a block and a half to reach the alley, he still kept working. Homelessness is not for the lazy. He'd panhandle as he walked.

"Spare some change?"

"Why, so you can take it back to your condo and use it to make payments on your BMW?"

This was one of the most common urban myths he encountered. As far as he could tell, it had no basis in fact whatsoever, but there were a lot of people who believed that beggars were secretly rich. They had stock market portfolios and fancy cars. Their wives were beautiful and their children well scrubbed. Why would rich people disguise themselves as homeless, and panhandle in the street? Because beggars make huge amounts of money. It was better than currency speculation or alfalfa futures.

Of course, the story was complete bullshit. Maybe there were one or two crazy people who had lots of money, and *enjoyed* begging, and perhaps a reporter followed up on them, did a thorough investigation and discovered that they were fake. Maybe, just maybe, this had happened once or twice. However, he knew the story was so full of shit, it stank.

Rich people could always prove they had a lot of money. They could show you their bank balance, their bank statements, their reports from their stockbrokers, and even had wads of cash they could take out of their pockets and wave under your nose. If you were rich, you could prove it.

You couldn't prove it if you were poor; well and truly broke, and had nothing in the world but what you had with you. You couldn't show them a bank statement with a zero balance even if you still had an account in your name. How can you prove that you didn't have *another* bank account, with millions of dollars in it? It was easy to prove what you had, and impossible to prove what you didn't. Even if you have the proof, there would always be someone who would rather believe you were a secret millionaire with money in the Cayman Islands, and real estate in your wife's name, than think about giving you fifty cents. He replied:

"No, man. I don't have a condo, and I traded my Beemer for automatic weapons a long time ago, and now I can't remember where I put my AR-15."

Homeless: A Day in The Life.

His heckler was surprised that he answered back. Usually, our friend would've ignored a comment like that, but it was good to respond once in a while, just to show a little backbone.

"Yeah, you guys always have more money than you let anyone know about."

That *was* true. If you had ten dollars in your pocket, you kept your mouth shut about it, so that no one would try to borrow any of it from you.

His response was simple, "Bullshit. Fuck off." He looked his heckler, a white man in his 20s, in the eye. The man just walked away. No victory for or against the urban legend today. Nothing he could say would change the man's mind. Beggars, the homeless, and street people were rich. Fantastically wealthy, and every one of them was trying to cheat everyone in the world out of whatever they could get. He owned Argentina. He owned the sky.

He decided that *this* homeless man wasn't going to tap into his enormous savings. Instead, he would fill out his portfolio by doing some more dumpster diving. "Sell everything I have in Amazon. Now."

It was surprising how many people stopped to ridicule him. They seemed to enjoy it, even though it was pointless. It seemed that most people already knew all about the homeless, whether they knew anything or not. Most folks were sympathetic and at least a little compassionate. A few, however, thought homeless people were all dishonest, lying, cheating, lazy, drunken human garbage. There was nothing anyone could say to change their beliefs. Neither group knew what they were talking about. They made up their minds, and carved their opinions in granite. Those who had sympathy for the homeless and those who wanted them herded into concentration camps were both equally ignorant. Neither had any idea what life was really like for those on the street.

He gave his head a short but forceful shake as if to drive these thoughts from his mind. There was no point in staying irritated at the heckler. There were garbage dumpsters waiting for him, and one of them might have the British Crown Jewels. "You never know."

He kept walking. He came to an alleyway that had a mix of trash from apartments and small stores. As he looked into it, he saw the flashing lights of a cop car at the far end. However temporarily, this was police territory, so he continued on to the next block and turned into the alley there. No cops. He could see that a couple of dumpsters were so full they wouldn't close properly, and knew the trash hadn't been collected there for several days; maybe a week. That made them stinky, but it also put the recent trash close to the top, where it was easier to get at.

Opening the first one, he saw a paper bag from Jack-in-the-Box. His first thought was that there might be something he could eat, but when he looked inside, he saw that there was no food in it, and the weight was from a bunch of condiments at the bottom. That was a good find, but not a great one. He took out a plastic packet of ranch dressing, another of ketchup, and a few salt packets. He used a napkin from the bag to wipe some ketchup off the ranch dressing packet. They went into one of the pouches on the outside of his backpack. It was especially useful. It could turn all sorts of otherwise unpalatable foods into something worth eating. If he had ranch dressing, then he wasn't averse to buying some vegetables. In the grocery stores, the smallest size bag of salad usually cost $1.20. If he had some salad dressing, he could just tear open the salad bag, pour it in, shake the bag around, and eat it. If he had any other food to go with it, even a piece of bread, then it was a meal. A small one, but still a meal. It was always a good idea to keep some salt on hand. It was one of those things that was never around when you needed it, and he prided himself on his ability to be ready for anything.

Kentucky Fried Chicken bags were special. Half the time, they had those little alcohol-based cleaning towels, in their tinfoil wrappers. Those were really good for washing up. You could wipe your face with one of them, and it would actually be clean. He took every one he saw. Their food trash was usually some of the worst. Somehow, he could bring himself to eat a hamburger that someone had already taken a bite from, but he couldn't bring himself to do that with a piece of chicken. A hamburger was supposed to have a bun on the outside, and that made it reasonably dry. The surface of the meat in a chicken breast was moist, and somehow that made hand-me-down chicken disgusting. He knew there was a risk of picking up a disease from any food like that, and meats could go bad pretty quickly. He stopped noticing how gross his food was years ago. But that didn't matter. His aesthetics, and his feelings of disgust, not microbiology, decided what he would eat and what he wouldn't. It wasn't the only thing in his life that made no sense.

He kept on going through the dumpster, and found a bag half-full of black jellybeans. That was an exciting find for him. He had a passion for black jellybeans. When he was a kid, he would get them on Easter, and sometimes he got some at Halloween. A bag of mixed flavor jellybeans would usually have just a few black ones, and when he was young, that was the only way he could get them. Just a few at a time. A whole bag of them was a real luxury. A desert for emperors. He saw the displays of jellybeans in the grocery store, but it would never have occurred to him to actually buy some, even if they were all the black kind. He just wouldn't have thought of it. The jellybeans went into his coat pocket. "Black is beautiful."

He rooted through the dumpster some more, but didn't see anything special. Makeup containers, with only the last residues in the corners. Ordinary kitchen trash. Cereal boxes. Old herbal tea bags. An empty bottle of soy sauce. A carton of hazelnut coffee creamer gone bad. A crushed coffee cup from Starbuck's (he saw a lot of those), and another empty coffee cup, including the lid, from 7-Eleven. He kept that, of course. Anything in a clean 7-Eleven cup could be reheated in their microwave for free. Once he even heated some chicken wings that way.

He carried on to the next dumpster, but it had nothing of any interest or value. He racked his brains to remember what day of the month it was, and realized that it was only four or five days from the first, when people moved. That meant that there was a chance for "moving out trash." That was the unique kind of garbage that appeared when people moved out of their apartments. Pieces of furniture; all the old cans of stuff in the kitchen that somehow people bought, but never got around to eating and usually, a lot of clothes. Sometimes there were little statues, vases, and other pieces of art. Those always made good street sale items. Even though he'd been trash picking on and off for the whole day, he hadn't seen even one good pile of "moving out trash." Never mind. Some months, lots of people moved. Other months, almost no one did, but for the next few days, the trash would have more potential than usual.

Another dumpster. The cover of a celebrity magazine promised to tell him which movie stars had boob jobs, and he tossed it aside, disgusted with himself. He liked breasts as well as any man, but they were out of his reach in more ways than one, and it did him no good to reflect on it. Any priest, nun, or monk who wanted advice on how to keep their vow of celibacy could come to him. He'd know *just* what to tell them.

He kept looking in the dumpsters. He looked inside, and saw some leftover Chinese food. He left it alone. There were also some unused disposable chopsticks, and he took two pairs. They were always handy to have. The crackheads in the park needed sticks to push the screens, made of a piece of brass Brillo pad, to just the right depth in their glass pipes. He didn't smoke crack, so he wasn't sure why they were always doing this, but they did, and one pair of chopsticks would be good to eat with, and the other would provide a couple of "pushers" for a crackhead. He knew lots of them, and even though their paths didn't cross too much, it was always good to be friends with everyone in the park. Giving a crackhead the little stick they needed to smoke their "rocks" was one way to keep on their good side. Besides, when he saw someone smoking crack, asking them if they needed a pusher opened the way for him to ask for a smoke.

He found a rosary, made of blue plastic. He took it along, even though he wasn't Catholic. It made a plausible good luck charm, and if he saw a Mexican in the park, he could ask them if they wanted it. And he could also choose one who was having a cigarette, and then ask for one. There were lots of Mexican homeless in the city, and they were always good people, even when they were drunk. Of course, many of them could go back to Mexico and live with their families. Maybe knowing that your family would welcome your return was enough to make the streets bearable. He saw groups of them sitting in their corner of the park, and they were always either laughing, or talking quietly. No fights, and no screaming. They left Mexico to earn money in America to send back to their families. Success was imperative for them. Their machismo and honor both demanded it. Like masterless samurai, and they accepted their situation philosophically. They believed in the Holy Mother, the Queen of Heaven and her immaculate conception. She would help them. "Hail

Mary, Full of Grace."

Our friend was finding things, and he was keeping them, but so far nothing he could sell had turned up. That was the point of his being there, and he started getting a little frustrated. The morning's luck was not repeating itself now.

He kept going, and found a half pint bottle of vodka, with about two fingers worth still at the bottom. That was really useful. He didn't like getting drunk, but a good stiff one just after he got in his sleeping bag helped him to sleep through the night. It was even about the right amount. He squeezed it into the main compartment of his backpack, to use his spare pants as padding for it. Now all he had to do was remember it when it was time to sleep.

Still, nothing really good. Nothing he could turn into cash.

The next dumpster had a box of books, all nonfiction and looking fairly new. They were worth money, but books were heavy, and the secondhand bookstores often weren't buying anything. They'd have a sign in the window that said, "No buying today." Most of the time, it was just because the manager wasn't there that day, and they insisted on doing all the buying themselves.

He took the box of books out of the dumpster and looked around for a place where he could hide them until the next day. Then, he could stop in the bookstore to check whether they were buying that day before he invested the effort of carrying them down. They usually wouldn't buy every single book, but it was equally rare for them to refuse them all. They were sure to want *"US-Russia Relations, 1995 to 2015."* Books were good business.

A box full of good titles could bring in enough to live for the entire day without doing anything else. The tourist market had two used bookstores, and whatever he couldn't sell to the first one, he could take to the other, who didn't pay as much. They had seen him enough times over the last few years that they knew he wasn't a thief, and he was educated enough to know which books had a market and which ones didn't. "No Harlequin romances." He also knew the rules for selling books. If the book dealer said no, that was it. There was no appeal, and he asked for none. If the bookseller said a specific copy of *"The Grapes of Wrath"* wasn't in good enough condition, then it went back into the box without another word. So the book buyers knew that he was easy to do business with. They always looked at his stuff, unless they were very busy, in which case, true to his word, he would come back again later.

So he needed a place to put the books where they would stay dry and unmolested until the next day. He made the simplest choice. He put them in another dumpster; one that belonged to an art supply store on the ground level, with apartments in the floors above it. The art supply store's dumpster was almost empty. It had probably been emptied that day, and it would be a few days until it was emptied again. The books would probably still be there. He closed up the box, but didn't have any packing tape to seal it shut. Of course. Who carries packing tape with them? He took some large black plastic garbage bags from one of the other dumpsters, and spread them out over the box of books. The next step was to get enough dry, clean garbage from the other dumpsters to bury it. He found a bag of trash that looked just right. It was large, but lightweight, and felt like it was mostly paper. That was perfect. He opened the bag and dumped its contents over his carton of books. It was as safe as he could make it,. The art supply store's name was on a sign above the back door, making it easy for him to remember where he was, so he could retrieve the box the next day.

He moved on to another dumpster.

Incredibly, this one had a bicycle it. He didn't know the brand name, but it looked expensive. I mean, really fucking expensive, Man. He had to take off his backpack to get into the dumpster, and once he was inside, he saw that he'd have to move a lot of garbage out of the way to get the bicycle out easily. Some trash pickers would have just thrown it on the ground, but that could get him a ticket for littering that he wouldn't be able to pay. So he climbed out again, and opened the dumpster next to it, then climbed back in and threw a few bags of trash from one dumpster to the next. In just a couple of minutes, he had excavated the bicycle well enough to lift it out, and drop it carefully on the ground.

He climbed out of the dumpster and began to inspect it. Before he finished, he realized that he wasn't wearing his backpack, and had no reason to leave it off. His infinite protectiveness towards his small bag of things rivaled that of a mother towards her child. It was everything he owned in the world. He shouldered his pack and kept on studying the bike. It looked like a racing type, with thin wheels and a narrow seat. He was getting on it to give it a test ride when he realized that the seat was too high for him. He got off, and opened its retaining ring, forced the seat down, closed it up again, and got on. This time, it was much more comfortable for him, but it's narrow seat pressed painfully against his ass.

The bicycle presented both a problem and a blessing. There was no lock for it, and that meant he had to keep it with him until he sold it. Someone would steal it if he left it anywhere and naturally, he had no way to prove it was his. For all he knew, a man's wife had gotten angry with him about how much time he spent on his bike, and put it in the dumpster to teach him a lesson. Now, when the poor fellow came home from work and found it was missing, and his wife told him it was in the rubbish, he would come out and find it gone. *That* would make him love her more, and teach him to spend more time with her. He knew that just taking it out of the bin wasn't enough to make it his, because anyone could challenge him about anything. It didn't seem very likely. The stuff in the trash was abandoned property, but you never got a receipt when you took something out of a dumpster. He had to get out of that alley soon, or else someone might appear, demanding that he give it back.

He didn't know of any bicycle stores right downtown.

The nearest one he could think of was about 5 miles away; maybe a little less. But he wouldn't ride it all that way unless he was sure that he could sell it, and there was a law that said you had to wear a helmet when you rode a bike. He didn't have one. He wasn't in a position to demand a good price from the shop. Everything about him said he would take nearly any offer.

He figured his best bet was to go back to the park and walk around saying "Anybody need a bicycle?", and then try to make whatever deal he could with anyone who seemed interested. He knew the odds weren't bad.

The other thing that helped him decide to ride it was that he could get to the park in just a few minutes that way. His feet hurt, and any plan that meant he didn't have to walk was a good one. He'd forgotten about his still-valid bus transfer. He climbed on and started to ride. He hadn't thought about how the gears should be adjusted, and they were all wrong for him. He started to peddle it, and in just a few seconds he, his backpack, and the bicycle all came crashing down. It saddened him to see that the sleeve of his coat was badly scraped. It hadn't been torn open, so it would still be warm, but it looked bad. His warm coat had crossed the line and he'd have to find another one eventually. Never mind. He didn't have to think about that today, but he did have to decide about the bicycle. He adjusted the gears, and cranked the peddles around by hand, until the bike responded and the wheels turned the way he thought they should. He got on it again, and this time he could ride it. It had been quite a while since he been on a bike, but what people said was true. You never forget how. Nevertheless, he wasn't sure he could ride it in traffic without getting hit by a car. He also didn't have a helmet, and he knew it was illegal to ride without one. The safest way was to ride it through the alleyways, and walk when he crossed the streets, so the police wouldn't see him riding without a helmet, and he wouldn't get hit by a car. His plan worked fine.

In a few minutes, he was back at the park.

"Anybody need a bike?"

"Bike for sale!" "I got a good deal on a bike."

It took him only about five minutes to make his way through the park, hawking his bicycle, but there were no takers. He knew what the next step was, so he wasn't too disappointed. He walked into an alley close by, opened the first dumpster he saw, and took out a cardboard box. He tore one of the flaps off, and took out his oversize sharpie pen, the one he used to make his panhandling signs. He wrote:

4 SALE.
CHEAP.

The brand name on the bicycle was *Trek*. He sat down on a bench close to the entrance to the park, and just waited. He watched the people come and go. A few people looked at the bicycle, and it wasn't long before someone stopped.

Our friend said: "Hey man, that's a *Trek*. That's a good bike."

He didn't really know if it was, but it looked expensive and he was pretty sure it wasn't a second-rate brand, so he just took a chance, and it turned out he was right.

"Yeah. One of the best. How much you want for it?"

"60 bucks, and that's a *good* price."

"It is. That's cheap. Why are you selling it so for so little? Is it stolen?"

"No. It's not stolen." Our friend knew the truth was a little too strange to be believed. He found it in a dumpster, and that's how it was. But people usually don't understand just how generous the trash can be at times, so he decided it would be better to make up a story. Besides, it would give him a chance to hone his storytelling skills.

"My friend left town today, and it doesn't look like he's gonna be back for a while. His sister came up from LA to take him home, but there was no way to get the bike on the car, so he just gave it to me. Kind of a farewell gift."

"So why don't you take it to a bike shop?"

"Man, there ain't no way they're going to buy this bike from me if I walk in the store looking like this."

The man kept looking at the bike, and then said: "I just don't know. Let me think about it."

Our friend shrugged and said, "Okay. Fine."

Lots of people walking by looked at it, and in a few minutes another man stopped. He didn't ask any questions. He just said, "I guess you know how much you want for it."

"$60."

The man just nodded, and looked thoughtful. He too walked away. The price of $60 had been turned down twice, so our friend decided to bring it down to $50.

He called after the second man:

"How about fifty?" The fellow nodded, but kept walking away. From out of nowhere, the first guy appeared again, and asked:

"Would you take forty?"

"How about forty-five?"

The man stood there, thinking. In a few seconds another guy was squatting down next to the bike, giving it a close look. The guy who offered forty knew he didn't have long to make up his mind, or at least he *thought* he didn't.

"Okay. It's a deal. 45." He stuck out his hand to shake on it, and our friend took his hand. It was a deal. The fellow took out the money, handed it over, got on his bicycle, and rode away. Probably, it could have gone for a couple hundred dollars, but that was in the other world; the one with bank accounts, credit cards, monthly payments, credit ratings, and automatically deposited paychecks. It had nothing to do with the economy of the street, where one dollar today is like ten bucks next week. Money existed only in the present moment.

He was pleased with this sale, and he didn't mind that the law of averages said it would be a long time before something like that happened again. For a moment, he imagined an inspirational poster of a Hindu God holding up his hands in the delicate postures of Indian statuary, with a caption that said:

"Yesterday's money is gone. Tomorrow's money doesn't exist yet. Find peace in the money you have now."

'Live in the present, 'cause presents are free.'

"Om."

The first thing he did was get another nickel bag from Tate. By his own standards, he was really in the money at this point, and he had about 1.5 grams of pot.

Tate had noticed the bicycle deal, and said:

"Man, you are blessed today. How'd you get that bike, anyway?" Tate knew he wasn't a thief.

"I shit you not. I found it in a dumpster."

"Serious?"

"Yep. Over by the Salvation Army store. I was going to go into a different alley, and dive the dumpsters there, but there were cops in that one, so I went to the next one down, and that's where I found it."

"God put the cops in that one alley to guide you toward the blessing he had for you in the next one. God is good! He gave us this glorious creation, and he gave you a bike. What I want to know is who the hell gonna put a bike like that in the trash?"

"I dunno. Could be they just got a better one." He recalled his earlier speculation.

"Maybe some guy's girlfriend got mad at him and threw his bike away. Maybe the owner died. Really, I have no idea. People throw out all kinds of shit."

He remembered some of the strange things he'd found in the trash. A wheel chair. That went to a white-haired American Indian Vietnam vet in the park who had a wheelchair that was only held together by duct tape and hardware store retaining rings. Wheelchairs are hard to sell, too. Everyone who needs one already has one. He was happy to replace it, and it took months for that old Native American to stop saying thank you for it. That was good karma.

Another time, he found a laptop that was still on. He

got a fast twenty bucks for that. If the laptop didn't have any power, everyone would think it was broken, and he wouldn't have gotten a dime for it. This one was still on. Weird. Then there was the time he opened a dumpster to discover that there was only one thing in it. An enormous pink Easter rabbit, about seven feet tall. He knew why it was out in the trash. Only a crazy man would want to live with a thing like that. The real mystery was why anyone would buy it in the first place. Once he found a brand-new motorcycle helmet. He got all of five dollars for it.

Another time, he found a women's fur coat. He didn't know what kind of fur it was, but he imagined it was valuable. He'd found it too late at night to have any chance of selling it, and it had started to rain, and he knew it would be impossible to sell a wet fur coat, so he bartered it for half a pack of cigarettes from a woman with a face covered with the red sores that proclaimed a meth addiction. Probably she was a hooker, and there was no way she was going to pass up a fur coat. Most likely, she slept in cheap hotel rooms, and as he thought about it, he realized that she probably took the fur coat back to her room, let it dry, and then took it to a used clothing store the next day. He was sure she made a good profit, with only ten cigarettes invested in it, but that was better than nothing, and he had no way to protect it from the rain or get it dry.

"Yeah, man. I seen some weird shit in the trash."

He'd also seen some truly horrific things in

dumpsters. He once found a trash bag that looked like it was full of clothes, but when he tore the bag open to see what was inside, he was confronted with a dead dog. It's lifeless eyes, exposed fangs, and tortured expression made him drop it instantly, and get himself out of the dumpster as fast as he could. It was harmless, but it scared the shit out of him. He even rinsed his hands in a puddle of water, because nothing could be dirtier than that bag. Sure, somebody loved that dog, but you really shouldn't get rid of a dead one by putting it in a trash bag. "That 'jes ain't right."

Another time, he found about a dozen bags of human shit. They were in strange plastic bags that had adhesive cardboard with holes in the middle on one side. Probably, they were colostomy bags. He was completely down and out, but no way would he ever trade places in life with someone who has to shit into a bag. "Man, that's harsh."

Another time, a dumpster had provided him with a bottle of Viagra. It was expired, but a little personal experimentation showed him it was still good, and he kept them buried in his backpack for many weeks, "just in case." Condoms also turned up regularly, and he always kept one or two, also "just in case," but he knew the odds were against him. Really, they were little more than talismans, material symbols of his unrealistic fantasies, which prevented them from being *completely* impossible. "You never know."

There are many kinds of despair, and the one that came over him when he thought that he might never have sex again was especially tormenting.

Once he even found a box of four dozen condoms. They were worth money, but he just couldn't bring himself to walk through the park with a large box of Trojans, calling out "condoms for sale." That dog just wasn't gonna hunt. His degraded way of living had wounded his pride so badly that it might never recover, but there were some things even he wouldn't do.

Once he found a prosthetic leg. There *had* to be a story behind that.

He'd also heard stories of people finding bundles of cash and gold coins, diamond rings and things like that. But it never happened to him. At least, not yet. He wouldn't let himself doubt these stories completely, because it really wasn't impossible, and believing it *could* happen helped him keep a tiny fragment of hope alive in his mind. "Maybe tomorrow, I'll find a bunch of money." Such mistakes only happened during major cleanouts, like when someone moved out of an apartment building or died, and everything they owned went out in the trash. Landlords were ruthless, and throwing away things tenants left behind was part of their normal routine.

Tate handed him his nickel bag, as he slid the money onto the table.

"Thanks, man. Right on." Tate was a good man, although he was always in a hurry to get on with his business. He didn't encourage customers to hang around and talk, but he always made them feel welcome. Tate sold pot as an act of devotion to his Rastafarian God, and he didn't have that harsh gimmethefuckinmoney attitude that other pot sellers in the street had.

Marijuana was legal in his state, and had been for a couple of years, but the cannabis shops never sold less than 1 gram at a time. You had to have an ID to enter, and that kept the underground pot business going. In fact, the street prices were about the same. Tate was at risk for getting a ticket for selling pot without paying the taxes, but since legalization, the cops didn't much care. They'd grab you for smoking dope in public, but they didn't want to bother with everyone who just happens to have some pot, in *case* they were selling it and hadn't been paying the taxes. The police weren't very enthusiastic about working for the tax authorities. Once in a while, the city had a crackdown, and then they had to deal with it, but left to their own devices, they'd ignore it completely.

He was no longer sure how much pot he had, but he knew it was plenty. For today.

He rolled himself another cigarette, thinking he could buy an actual deck of weeds if he wanted, but he'd think about that later. Bugler was good enough for now. After about a year on the streets, and learning how to pick the trash, he'd given up the habit of spending all his money as soon as he got it. Today had been good - very good, but you never knew what tomorrow would be like. He'd seen too many days bring in nothing at all.

CHAPTER SIX

A woman came walking through the park, calling out "food stamps." He waved her over to him and asked how much. The answer came back. Fifty cents on the dollar, and her card still had twenty bucks on it. He made up his mind instantly and didn't haggle. A lot of people think that it's a common abuse of the food stamp program, but our friend knew better. It didn't happen very often, and when it did, he needed to take advantage.

"You mean you'll gimme twenty bucks in food stamps for 10 bucks in cash, right?" She said, yeah, that was the deal. They crossed the street to a gourmet grocery store with an ATM, and checked the balance. It showed up as $19.65. Close enough.

He handed over a ten dollar bill, and she gave him the card and the pin. That was easy. He knew he shouldn't take it to a major grocery store, because they were more likely to ask him to show his SNAP[ii] card, and of course, he didn't have one. He couldn't even apply for one because he didn't have an address. But there were lots of other grocery stores in the area where he could use it. He decided to go over to one of the health food stores in the public market and buy a large bag of trail mix. It was guaranteed food for more than a day.

Everyone noticed him as he went into the store and immediately turned away to look at something else. All except the man behind the counter who watched him every second. His dirty lumberjack coat and the sleeping bag attached to his backpack were badges that showed his caste, and he didn't like knowing that everyone was thinking, "Homeless guy. Avoid at all costs." The store was too upscale for his liking, but they had a good price on trail mix. Safeway was easier to deal with, because it didn't cater to rich people, but their price was a little higher. Besides, he'd have to walk more than a mile to get there. Our friend did what he always did in those moments; he headed straight to the trail mix, weighed it out, and went to pay immediately. The clerk could only suspect he had stolen something in the aisles he visited. If he didn't stop to look at anything he didn't want, then he wouldn't have had the time to shoplift anything, and the clerk was less likely to make trouble for him.

He got about four pounds of the kind with chocolate chips, nuts, and dried raisins. He triple bagged it. That used up the balance on the card, leaving him with about 30¢ on the card. Too little to buy anything.

The clerk was supposed to ask him to show his SNAP card, but didn't bother, because that would've kept him in the store longer. If the clerk *had* asked him, he would have started going through all of his pockets, one by one, looking for it, until the clerk lost patience, and told him to make sure he could find it next time. He knew if he came back to the same store later on with another card, the clerk would probably "forget" to ask him then, too. He threw the card in the trash can just outside their door, after first looking to see if there was anything worthwhile in it. There wasn't.

He left the store and trudged up the stairs to the street level. As he walked, he felt the weight of the bag of trail mix, and realized he might have bought a little too much. He decided he'd get another cup of coffee and then walk back to the park, and see if Nick was still there and wanted to eat something. He remembered an Eskimo (*Inuit*) saying he heard on TV some time before his life collapsed, "the best place to store extra food is in your friend's stomach." If Nick wasn't around, he'd offer some to Tate, who would appreciate the gift, and maybe go easy on him the next time he had absolutely no money and really needed to get high. Tate never gave credit, but he would give away small amounts of marijuana for free to people who'd been nice to him. Once Tate gave three full grams to a guy who had warned him about a couple of undercover cops making the rounds in the park. Tate was smoking, breathing out billowing clouds of marijuana smoke with a deep Rastafarian pride, and committing an act of *Public Intoxication*.

Tate was about to get busted, but he knew this guy who tipped him off, so Tate didn't get a ticket for smoking in public. He could also have gotten arrested, and that would mean the loss of his entire inventory. So, when Tate ran into the same guy the next day, he gave him three grams. Free. Tate told the story as a way to show his own generosity, but also to subtly put out the message that he rewarded people who protected him. "What goes around, comes around."

Our friend kept walking back towards the park and stopped in at the grimy grocery store that sold hot coffee to go. $1.25 poorer, he got back to the park with the huge bag of trail mix, and started looking around for Nick.

He saw him over to one side, sitting at a picnic table with a group of black men between their 20s and 40s. Nick was not only black, he was *African*, and that gave him a symbolic status for some black folks. Besides that, he was over seventy, earning him the respect that comes with age. Nick spoke a few languages (including Swahili, Arabic and Dutch, from his days in the import export business), and they all knew about how he had been in three wars. "In fuckin' *combat*, man." Nick got respect.

"You come back here again, my brother." Nick always called him "my brother," when he was hanging out with other people, to make sure everyone knew they were friends, and he wouldn't have to listen to questions like "Who's the white guy?"

"Hey, man. I just had me some good luck. I found a bicycle in a dumpster. No shit, a fuckin' bike, man. I sold it for forty-five bucks. You want to eat something?"

"Sure, man. What you got?"

"Trail mix, from the health food store."

"Okay. Gimee some."

Our friend looked around, and counted five people already sitting at the table besides Nick and himself. His bag of trail mix wouldn't last long with seven people eating it. Keeping his back to the table so they wouldn't see what he was doing and how much he really had, he took it out, and put about a third of it in another plastic bag. He packed up the larger one, and put it in his bag. Putting the smaller one on the table, he said, "Go on. Have some if you want." The men at the table gave him an appreciative nod, and a quiet chorus of 'Thank yous' went around the group.

He sat down next to Nick, and the youngest one at the table said, "Why you sittin' down here?" Before anyone could answer, Nick spoke up, "This is my good friend, man. Don't make no trouble, okay?" and reached for our friend's coffee. He took a sip and handed it back, and our friend also drank a little. It was really to show that they would drink from the same cup, and were therefore close friends.

He wasn't going to share his pot because he didn't have enough for seven people. They started eating the trail mix, and he took it as a symbolic gesture of acceptance. In spite of the strong stress and tension about race among the homeless, he was invited to join their group for a while. He recognized a couple of the men there as regulars in the park, and they told the youngest to shut up, saying, "He's cool." It didn't mean he was cool: stylish and admirable. It meant that our friend was *cool*, an okay person, not a racist, and like any other sensible mammal, had nothing to do with the cops if he could help it.

One of them, a man in his 30s, and clearly homeless, continued the conversation they were having before our friend arrived.

"Man, that motherfucker was *cold*. He hit me on the foot 'fore I could even do what he was tellin' me to do. He jus' up 'n hit me with his stick. He say I hafta' move on, an' 'fore I could say anything, he jus' started beatin' on my feet. Man, that motherfucker was *cold*."

He was talking about a cop. Everyone seemed to have some kind of horror story to tell about them. Most of the cops were good, and most of the time, they didn't resort to violence just to make a point. But they turned brutal once in a while. Nobody knew why. Of course if they did know why, they could take steps to avoid it.

"Was that the one with the scar on his eyebrow?"

"Yeah, that's the one."

Nick spoke up, "That's officer Stanyan. That guy's a motherfucker. He just do like that."

"Dey all like dat."

Nick argued with him. "No, not *all* of them. Some is good."

"Dey all hate us."

One of the other men spoke up, "No man, dey all hate *you*." Everybody laughed.

"Bullshit. 'Dey ain't got no reason to hate me. I don' make no trouble for dem. I don' do nuttin. *Nuttin.*"

Our friend started talking, but was rapidly silenced by a storm of sudden conversation, with everyone talking at once.

Nick spoke up for him, "You tell us why they do like that."

"They get the word from City Hall. Time for a crackdown, and then you step out of line, and they fall on you like a fuckin' house."

There seems to be a basic assumption in Western civilization. If you weren't doing anything wrong, then you weren't supposed to be punished. Or hassled. Or intimidated. Even if there was no justice in the world, some things were supposed to be fair.

Nick demanded to know, "Why you think they care so much?"

Our friend answered, "I think it's the real estate business. Urban properties ain't worth as much with homeless people on the sidewalks. Companies will pay a little more rent for an office in a building without any homeless on the street. Maybe it's just a little more, but the landlords get it every month, and they get it from hundreds of tenants. If somebody has a building worth a billion dollars, it's going to rent out for, I don't know, another 5% if there's no homeless people around, you get me? 5% of $1 billion is *fifty million dollars*, so it's worth it for them to bribe the people on the City Council to crack down on the homeless wherever they're puttin' up new buildings or trying to rent out them fuckin' high-priced offices. Y'know; 'campaign contributions'."

Right now, anywhere "they're puttin' up new buildings" meant the whole downtown area.

He continued, "So you got a bunch of different cops, standing in their meeting room, and their boss is telling them they got to be more aggressive with the homeless. The good ones ignore him, and the sadistic ones think 'now they got their chance'. Next thing you know, they think they it's *okay* to start beatin' on street people. Some of them act that way all the time, 'cause that's just their personality. Some of 'em *like* it. Nobody who wants to be nice to people ever becomes a cop. Listen, man, who the fuck takes a job that means they have to put people in cages? Seriously, what kind of people wanna do that; you know what I'm saying?"

The group went silent for a moment, and then all five started talking at once, "You got dat right." "Amen to that." "Mm-hmm."

Homeless: A Day in The Life.

The pound of trail mix on the table was almost gone. The youngest one ate handfuls, one after the other. He must've been hungry. No one said a word about it.

The plain fact was that this city had more poor people than it had low-income housing for them, and the poorest were squeezed out into the street. Thousands of cheaper apartments had been razed to make way for high-rise offices and condos, populated by yuppies, who drank Starbuck's coffee, did "Netflix and chill," kept a cat, and spent their remaining time either shopping, having sex, or eating neatly-packed food, delivered to their door, with one convenient click on their cell phones; artsy napkins included.

During the Nazi era, Germans who answered "apartment for rent" ads in the newspaper never knew the previous occupants had been incinerated in Auschwitz. The yuppies who moved into the city over the last couple of years never knew that ordinary working people lost their cheaper homes so someone could offer them expensive and elegant urban rentals. They had no reason to ask. The young urban professionals were remarkably obtuse about life among the poor. It seemed like they should know, but they didn't, and they didn't want to. Their landlords certainly weren't going to tell them. The spiral, climbing ever upwards, rested on the destroyed homes of poor people.

The trend was continuing, and every year there were more homeless people on the street, as more yuppies moved into the city. The higher value of their apartment buildings meant that the city could levy a higher property tax. It also meant that the profit-per-square-foot of the cities' land was skyrocketing, and real estate developers were making huge amounts of money. It seemed there wasn't a square inch of the city that didn't have real estate developers watching it. Together, they comprised a ruthless, hungry beast. As the developers worked the city over, more and more people were pushed out. None of the construction magnates wanted to build housing that rented for a few hundred dollars a month. They were hungrier than that, and built large apartment and office buildings with scores of stainless steel and glass units, each of which rented out for thousands.

Our friend, like all other homeless people, had a love/hate relationship with the "yuppies", the young urban professionals. On the one hand, the wave they were riding had turned mere poverty into total destitution for so many people. If they could rent a room for a couple of hundred dollars a week, the way it used to be, they wouldn't be homeless. Even the drunks and the drug addicts could mostly manage to get indoors in those days. If you have a $40 a day drug habit, then you have to find $1200 a month just for your drugs. You need to find about as much for your food and everything else. If you add $2000 a month to that for a room to live in, you just can't do it. If a rented room costs $800 a month, then most of the time, you'll be able to pay the rent, one way or another. If it's a choice between paying the rent and buying drugs, a true drug addict will let the rent go unpaid, but most of the time, it doesn't happen that way.

Like everybody else, the very poor could manage to get by whether they were addicts or not. But when every entrepreneur under the moon is trying to get the market share where the big bucks are, few developers will say to themselves: 'There are 7000 homeless people in this city. How can I make money from that?' The obvious answer would be to build cheap housing, but the stringent building codes and rising land values in big cities meant the numbers no longer added up. Urban regulations will have to change before rooms for poor people become profitable again. With so few real estate developers even looking at low income housing, not many were lobbying for it at City Hall, and the ones that did, didn't have the same kind of money for campaign contributions that real estate developers had.

Our friend sat there, listening to the conversation, but didn't really feel like saying much more. He felt ashamed for having ended up on the streets, even as he placed the blame on "the system." He knew his own actions helped put him on the street, but once he'd lost *everything*, it no longer mattered whose fault it was. He would've loved to have climbed out of the hole he was in, but the rungs at the bottom of the ladder had rotted away, and there was nothing to hold on to. The idea of getting out of the pit on his own seemed ridiculous. Of course, the Veteran's Administration wouldn't help. As far as they were concerned, none of his problems were related to his military service. They told him to come back when he was old enough to qualify for free medical care when he was sixty-five. That was years away. The tangle of regulations, policies, schedules of benefits, limitations and the shelves filled with manuals made it all so complicated that he had to accept what the caseworker said.

The conversation turned to hip-hop music, and neither he nor Nick knew anything about it, or even liked it very much. Nick liked the music from his home country, and also reggae. Our friend leaned over to Nick and said "mujawan," which was their private code for pot. It imitated the way Nick sometimes mumbled the word marijuana, voicing the silent 'J.' Nick understood. It was time to go somewhere and smoke a bowl, without having to get five other people high. That runs into money.

It was getting late in the day, and our friend really didn't want to do anything more, and there wasn't anywhere to go. The panhandling hadn't been bad, and the trash picking was great. It was time to take a break.

They moved across the park, to another bench; one that was right on the street, and sat down again. There was still some coffee left.

He filled their pipes, more generously than earlier, and they started smoking. Nick had a coughing fit, so they had to stop, because if the cops heard that characteristic hacking cough, they might walk over and start talking about public intoxication. Not good. He stood up, and looked around, "scanning for hostile life forms." No cops around. Nick always said he was too paranoid about the police, but our friend had never been arrested while living on the streets, and he relied on his own operating procedures, no matter what anyone said.

Nick seemed to have a magic personality. His accent and demeanor gave him a certain rough disarming charm, and no one thought he could be a threat to anyone. Nevertheless, he probably killed more people in his guerrilla fighter days than anybody else in the park, no matter how violent their past. His private death toll included scores of victims. He was a warrior, but didn't talk about it very much.

"Man, you too afraid about the police. They ain't looking for you and they don't give a fuck about a couple of people smoking pot."

Our friend didn't believe it for a second.

Nick told him a story about how a policewoman had caught him with a crack pipe, and when she asked him if he had any crack, he told her "no," and asked how old she was. "You too young to be police. How old are you?" He kept telling the policewoman how young she looked, stepping into his special "dumb African" personality. Eventually, she smiled and told him she'd forget about it if he put the glass pipe on the ground, next to a storm drain, and just crush it with his foot. As Nick told the story, that's what he did, and she let him go. She never even searched him.

"She just didn't want to arrest a 74-year-old man. You're just less trouble for her out here than you ever would be in the police station."

"Maybe you right. I think she liked me." Nick smiled.

Nick loved to tell stories about how well he got along with people. He met the president of Zaire, who gave him a complimentary room and free food at one of the biggest hotels in Kinshasa. He talked about how young women still flirted with him, and how rich businessmen in the jewelry trade still looked for him, to order gemstones from Tanzania. Nick had a rich past, both in money, and life experiences, but some of his stories obviously weren't true. You had to know the difference between a liar and a bullshit *artist* to appreciate Nick.

"Give me three dollars, my brother." The day had been good, and Nick was a friend, so he gave him the money. It would come back to him, for sure, the next time Nick got any. The money was for crack, and now that he had it, he was off to buy a little bit for his pipe. Probably, Nick was going for a five-dollar rock, and already had two bucks of his own. That meant that once he had smoked, Nick would have nothing at all in his pockets.

"You stay here? I be back soon." No problem.

He took out his book, and started to read, but then he remembered that he had tobacco, and started rolling a cigarette. He carefully avoided the gaze of another street person walking by, hoping to avoid a request for a smoke. With the tobacco out where anyone can see it, he couldn't pretend that he was about to run out, or that he was on his last cigarette. But the man surprised him.

"Can you spare me one of those papers?" He didn't want a cigarette, he just wanted one of the rolling papers.

"Sure, man. Here you go." That was easy, but he finished rolling his cigarette and put the tobacco away a little faster than usual. He enjoyed a moment of genuine serenity as he found himself stoned, having a smoke, drinking coffee, and actually reading a book. A police car went by, and the cops scrutinized him as they slowly drove past. They didn't stop. He never knew whether it was because he was doing something that caught their attention, they were just checking out everyone, or they were looking for someone in particular. Nevermind. There were some things he would never know.

He sat there for about 20 minutes before Nick came back, and it was easy to see that Nick had found some crack, and smoked it before he returned to their bench.

"I don't like to smoke crack in front of you. You always too paranoid about the cops."

"Hey, man, a couple of them went by in their car just a few minutes ago. You shouldn't do that shit sitting right on the street. You should make them work harder to see you smoking." Nick just nodded. Our friend was right, and he knew it. Avoiding absolutely *all* interactions with the police called for effort and strategy. Nick was getting a little lazy in his old age.

"Roll me one cigarette, my brother."

He'd have to get some more Bugler. It was running low. He thought it would last longer than it did, but that was no problem. There was money, and the 24-hour 7-Eleven carried it, so he could get more any time.

They sat on the bench a while longer, and Nick said "I been here all day, and I'm gonna go home. I'm old, you know that? It makes me tired."

"Yeah, right."

Nick shuffled away, and our friend sat there a while longer, reading his book. Reading made his mind quiet and muted his restlessness. It cut down on the depressing thoughts and helped him stop feeling like he was missing out on something when he sat and did nothing. He stayed there with his book for a while, until he got that nagging feeling that said it was time to get up and *do* something.

He remembered that he had some black jellybeans, so he opened them up, and ate a few of them. Eating them was less exciting than he thought they would be, and they were made of nothing but sugar. Remembering this, he realized he hadn't brushed his teeth that day.

The coffee was finished. It was too soon for another cigarette, and he was getting restless. He put on his backpack, and made his way to the public restroom again, where he brushed his teeth with hot water. He didn't have any toothpaste, but he figured that the hot water would dissolve the sugar from the trail mix and jellybeans now attacking his neglected teeth. Someone came in to use a urinal while he was there, but it didn't bother him very much, because brushing your teeth was one thing you could do in a public bathroom that made you seem like you were at least trying to be clean. However, he was in a public bathroom, and he thought it best to take advantage of it while he was there.

He sat down on the toilet, and after a couple of minutes, which he spent reading his book, another discharge, much more peaceful than the last ones, made him feel he was finally done with the spoiled shrimp from the day before.

He washed his hands, grateful that no one had come in over the last couple of minutes, and puzzled over what he should do next. It was getting late in the day, and that meant that sitting with his sign ("Brother, can you spare a dime?" - A classic) probably wouldn't work. That kind of panhandling was only effective when there was a lot of foot traffic, and there was always a heckler who would give him just one dime.

The new socks from the Salvation Army store earlier that day came to mind, so he sat down on a bench just outside the men's room. He took off his shoes, and peeled off his outer socks, noticing their smell, and that each one had a hole in the heel. He had put on his new ones, and started putting his shoes on again, when a couple of security guards came.

"You hanging around here?"

"No, Sir. I'm just tying my shoelaces, and then I'll be on my way." He didn't want to imply that he'd been changing his clothes there, even if it was just his socks. Normal people didn't do that.

The guards could see that he only had one shoe on, so they knew he was doing more than just tying his shoelaces. They gave him an irritated look, and went into the men's bathroom. It looked like they were just doing their rounds of the place, but he worried that maybe someone had complained while he was in there brushing his teeth, and they had gone to see if there was any problem. He got his other shoe on quickly, but still tied the laces with care, because his feet would hurt more if he didn't. He wanted to get out of there fast, hoping to be gone before the guards came out. The less they saw him, the less they would think about him. He was on his way out before they left the men's room. The new socks felt good.

Over the years, he had gained an almost ninja-like power of invisibility, letting him stay out of sight when he wanted to. There were safe places, and there were dangerous places. The bench where he changed his socks was surrounded by small shops, and the shopkeepers were never fond of the homeless. It was in a kind of gray area between safety and danger, but it was a place where he could sit down, and that made it worth the risk for a few minutes. It wasn't a good place to hang out. Besides, it was indoors. Smoking was forbidden, and that alone was enough to keep homeless people from loitering there, unless it was raining. Even then, places like that only offered a temporary respite, but you could usually get away with grabbing a few paper towels from the bathroom, and using it to dry off your hair and wipe your face.

Rainy days were bad days.

He congratulated himself for remembering to change his socks while he was still indoors. Besides the benches in the market buildings and the park there was almost no place to sit down these days. Any ledge that was the right height to sit on had turned hostile. Now they had metal strips with jagged teeth so it was painful to sit on them. Now there were cobblestones embedded in the concrete beneath highway overpasses, making it impossible to sleep there. Newer awnings over stores had gaps in them, to let the rain fall through, so that the homeless wouldn't find any shelter under them.

The benches had been removed from the sidewalks all over the city. The homeless would gather anyplace on the street that was even a little comfortable. Landlords and real estate developers who complained that this lowered the value of their property found cooperative ears at City Hall. The simplest way to keep the homeless from hanging out on city benches was to take them out. Not many people noticed, because the process was slow and gradual, but there was nowhere to sit on the city streets anymore, except right on the ground, and even that could get you a ticket for loitering. Some parks had been completely taken over by homeless people because there wasn't anywhere else for them to go. They couldn't just keep walking. Eventually, they have to stop and rest somewhere, and the parks were the only places left. Real estate magnates walked past, looking at the bums, wondering how to make them all go away.

Technically, the police were supposed to ask you to "move along" before they hit you with a loitering ticket, but he had heard a few stories where they had just walked up to a vagrant, and handed them one, or just arrested them. Like most tales of police abuse he heard on the street, it was plausible, but they always came from someone who heard it from someone who was there. He could never be sure if they were really true.

Loiter:
"To linger or hang around in a public place or business where one has no particular or legal purpose. Loitering is a crime, punishable by a fine not to exceed $500.00 or by confinement in the county or other jail, county correctional institution, or such other places as counties may provide for maintenance of county inmates, for a total term not to exceed 6 months, or both."

Our friend had never been arrested for anything, but he heard stories about people getting busted for loitering, and he suspected that the real reason was that they gave the cops too much trouble. The loitering charge was a convenient way to bust them. When that happened, they usually added "disorderly conduct." to the charges. By the time it got to court, the loitering charge was dropped, but the street person could still have to face the disorderly conduct charge. Naturally, in most cases, they would have never been disorderly if the police had just left them alone in the first place.

It was one of the perennial mysteries of homeless life, "Why don't they just leave me alone? I ain't makin' no trouble. I'm just sittin' here." There were reasons why the police wouldn't just leave people alone, but the homeless never knew what they were, and the cops never told them. The police had the badge, though, as Nick pointed out several times:

"The badge is just a symbol for the gun."

Our friend heard that some cities had even passed laws making it illegal to sit on the sidewalk because there was no way to make the street itself into a hostile environment. You could get a ticket just for sitting down. "Man, that's *cold*."

The alleys still had plenty of doorways with a step or two where you could sit down, and the police never enforced the loitering laws there. In the alleyways, the homeless were never in the way of the yuppie office workers, the tourists, or the real estate developers (who felt they were losing money every time they saw anybody who was destitute).

Our friend walked through the alleyways, opening the dumpsters and looking inside as he went along. They had already yielded him a bag of Hello Kitty toys and a bicycle. Together, they brought him $65 in one day. His luck had been with him so far. "You never knew." He would keep on looking.

It was getting dark, and that made dumpster diving more difficult, so he focused on the ones that were illuminated by security lights, but they were also covered by security cameras.

He mused to himself, "These people are so rich that they install cameras to watch their *garbage*." He knew some trash pickers were clumsy and unprofessional. They would throw trash on the ground from the top of a dumpster so they could get at what was underneath. He knew better, and always cleaned up after himself, leaving nothing that would bother the video cameras. Tossing garbage on the ground invited the buildings' janitors to come out and yell at them, and you could get a ticket for littering or "creating a public nuisance."

Littering:
"Knowingly and improperly placing trash or refuse so as to be or create a nuisance or health concern on any public or private property."

Creating a Public Nuisance:
"Acting to bring about a condition which is injurious to health or offensive to the senses, or an obstruction to the free use of property, so as to interfere with the comfortable enjoyment of life or property, or unlawfully obstructs the free passage or use, in the customary manner, of any public park, square, or street."

He kept going. He found a box of little pods of coffee; the kind used in fancy coffee machines, but decided not to take them. You could only sell things like that if you were having a street sale, and he didn't get the feeling that it would happen soon. Besides, if he took it, he'd have to carry it, and it was bulky. "Too bad."

For no particular reason, he decided to switch to another alley. He walked to the street, turned, and headed up to the next one, which he knew had only office buildings on each side. He always did better in alleys behind apartment buildings, but trash from offices and stores could also be interesting. They were more likely to have expensive electronics that were still in working condition, but the disadvantage was they were harder to sell, and were often too heavy to carry. He had left behind untold numbers of printers, FAX machines, monitors, telephones, and even entire computers. Most of them worked just fine, and they were only replaced because the company upgraded their hardware. It was an endless cycle. Today, a state-of-the-art computer might sell for a couple of thousand dollars, and in just three or four years, it would be considered obsolete, and any computer store he brought it to would tell him it was almost worthless. When he had something, it was trash. After he sold it to a merchant, it became a treasure. The waste that surrounded him was appalling, but it was also the source for a little more than half of all the money he got.

Todd Murphy

CHAPTER SEVEN

He walked into another alley and saw that part of it was a complete mess. For a moment he thought about finding another one, behind a different street so that no one would blame him for it, but he had a feeling he should go through it anyway. When he got to the section with trash all over the ground and cardboard boxes dissolving in puddles of water, he could see that it was behind a restaurant. Its back door was open, and he could hear the kitchen workers, talking in Spanish. It was busy that night.

He knew what to do. He knocked on the door and stood respectfully one step back from it. A well-groomed man in his early 30s appeared. He was wearing black pants, a white shirt, and an apron; the standard uniform for waiters in expensive restaurants. His expression changed the moment he saw our friend as he assumed that nothing but trouble would come from talking to him. But he had answered the knock, and couldn't just ignore him.

"What do you want?"

"Are you the manager?"

"Yeah, that's me." That was a lucky break. It would be harder if a waiter or dishwasher had answered the door.

"I can see the back of your restaurant is a mess, and I was wondering if you'd like me to clean it up for you. It looks like you're real busy tonight, and I thought you might be able to use a hand for a little while. I won't charge you much to do the job, and I could really use the work."

His reasoning made sense to the manager. He *was* having a busy night, and he was shorthanded. The mess had to be cleaned, but the only one to do it was the dishwasher, who would complain when they gave him the extra work. He was too busy to get away from the dishwashing machine, and the Board of Health regulations for restaurants didn't allow someone to go straight from cleaning an alley back to working in the kitchen.

"How much do you want?"

Our friend hadn't thought this through, but it was a restaurant, and they would probably give him a meal, or at least some fresh food in a "take out" container, on top of whatever cash they gave him. He knew that every restaurant manager, almost without exception, would claim they were willing to give food to a hungry man, if the guy just asked politely. That was better than ordering a meal and then skipping out on the check. It never actually worked out that way.

The managers either had nothing they could spare at that moment, or were too busy to think about it. They might say to come back later, but no one ever did. It was easier for a homeless person to just move on than to plan the rest of their evening around some bread and a salad that *might* come later on. Besides, most bums weren't in the habit of planning their days. They lived their lives an hour or so at a time.

"How about fifteen bucks?" The manager wasn't going to take time to negotiate. He was busy and needed a straightforward offer he could answer with either a yes or a no.

"How long do you think it will take?" Our friend just lied (he had no idea) and said:

"Maybe an hour (it really was a mess), but I'll get everything in the dumpsters, and get all those five gallon plastic cans stacked up nice. It'll look good when I'm done. Word of honor, man. You can pay me then. If you want me to sweep, you'll need to give me a broom."

The manager knew it probably wasn't going to take a full hour, but he couldn't be completely sure, and fifteen bucks was a cheap price to take the edge off the restaurant's workload that night. Besides, it would cost more than that for the dishwasher to do it on overtime pay.

"Okay. Just don't make a lot of noise while you're doing it. Never mind the sweeping."

Nobody ever swept out an alleyway, but his offer to do it made him look like a hard worker. The manager regretted his decision almost immediately. Some homeless were hard workers, and others seemed to create little dramas over everything, so there was no end to the petty hassles.

He worked for the restaurant now, even if it was only for a little while, so he could tuck his backpack behind the open back door, and no one could mess with it. Our friend began his work immediately. The wet, sloppy cardboard was the first thing he worked on. He began with the most disgusting job, because he knew it would make a quick and obvious change in the state of the alley. The manager was sure to glance out the door to see if he was working, and our friend wanted him to see visible progress.

The slimy cardboard got his hands dirty, but he was relieved to notice a water spigot behind one of the restaurant's three dumpsters where he could wash them. He made a mental note to remember it. He could fill his water bottle there when he needed to. Most water taps in alleyways were now under lock and key. Too many homeless people were using them without shutting them off completely. That was probably where the puddles that made the cardboard stew came from.

There were other cardboard boxes there. He broke them down so they lay flat, and put them in the recycling dumpster. By now, he'd been on the job for about twenty minutes. He saw an empty tin box that once held expensive chocolates, and put it in the garbage, where he noticed a couple of stained cotton restaurant napkins. They were dry, so he took them and put them on top of his backpack to clean his hands when he was finished. That way, he wouldn't need to ask to use the restaurant's bathroom. The idea with a job like this was to *get* the job and get started immediately. Once you began, they couldn't send you away without paying you *something*. However, if you appeared on the floor of the restaurant, as you usually had to do to reach the bathroom, they might tell you that you were done. They'd hand you less money than you'd agreed on, and tell you to go away. Homeless people had no place among their wealthy patrons. The idea was to make no trouble and keep it simple. That would make his boss happy and give him a better chance of getting a bonus meal when he was done.

While he was leaning over the last of the cardboard boxes, the manager stuck his head out the door, saw him working, and just said "Its lookin' good. Keep it up."

Now, the manager was convinced that he was a good worker, and might even start thinking about sending him away with a meal. "So far, so good." He had his trail mix, but he thought of it as reserve rations, and he'd try not to eat it when there was any other food available.

There were about a dozen white five-gallon plastic cans, the kind that held pre-made sauces or cooking oil, and had thick wire handles, and they presented a challenge. He had to pull the tops off them, and they weren't easy to open. All the same, he worked on them, one by one, until the tops were all removed. There were three of them that just wouldn't come off.

He had to take them further into the alley, so that when he laid them on their sides and jumped on them to force the lids off, the noise wouldn't go into the restaurant. They came off with a louder popping sound than he expected. By the time the manager stuck his head out the door to see what was going on, he was done with that, and was starting to rinse them out using the water. Each one took only a few seconds, and it wasn't really necessary, but they *looked* a lot cleaner, and that's what mattered to him. He was a trash picker, so he had a professional connoisseur's eye for garbage.

He stacked them up, nestling them inside one another. The loose pile of large plastic cans was now just three columns of white plastic. The lids went into the recycling bin. That was done.

There were a few plastic bags of trash that had to be put in the dumpsters, but they were too full to hold any more, so he climbed in after taking off his coat to protect it from the compost fermenting in there. As he was jumping lightly onto the trash to pack it down, he thought to himself that the manager would never be able to get the dishwasher to do the same thing. For the moment, the restaurant was better off with him.

There was a length of hose next to the spigot, with the sprayer at the end cut off. It wasn't very long. If it was a complete hose, someone would have stolen it, so it was cut down to where it was just barely serviceable. Our friend took a beer can from the dumpster, and wedged it into the doorway, so he could close the door partially and keep the water from splashing into the kitchen.

He hosed down the ground around the dumpsters, creating a rivulet that carried chunks of grease away from the back of the restaurant. The hose was on one side of the door, which was in the middle of their space on the alley, so he couldn't spray the whole area, but the manager wouldn't notice that unless he stepped out there and looked at the ground. The boss would probably just lean his head out and look around.

A little more than forty-five minutes had passed, and the job was done. In that city, it worked out to just slightly more than minimum wage for the time he had spent, but that economy had nothing to do with him. He enjoyed feeling useful for a while, and the amount of money he received was a lot more important than the number of minutes he gave. Besides, there wasn't much to do that time of day anyway, and the job prevented the crippling feeling of depressed boredom that could infect his evenings.

He decided to dawdle there long enough for a smoke, just so the manager felt he was getting his money's worth. He dried his hands on the stained, but otherwise clean, white cotton napkins, and then rolled another cigarette. He wet his finger in his mouth and held it up to check which way the wind was blowing. He stood downwind from the back door of the restaurant, and enjoyed his cigarette, combined with the feeling of accomplishment and a job well done.

It *was* well done. The pile of plastic cans was neat and organized, and the bags of garbage were now invisible. The ground was reasonably clean. The cardboard boxes were gone, and the dumpster lids now closed completely. Most noticeable of all, the "truck manure"; the soggy decomposing remains of cardboard boxes, was in the recycling bin where it belonged.

He stood there smoking, poised to hide his cigarette if the back door opened suddenly and throw it down quickly if the manager came out. He didn't want the boss to find him smoking on the job. Period.

About 50 minutes had passed since he first started work, and that was soon enough to announce that he was finished. He opened the back door and took out the beer can that prevented it from closing completely, and put it in the recycling bin, letting it slam shut so it would sound like he was still working. He knocked on the open door. This time, a Mexican kitchen employee answered. He wasn't sure if the guy knew he'd been working there or not.

"I finished cleaning up here. Can you ask the boss to come and check my work?"

"Hokay. I get heem for you."

It took a couple of minutes for the manager to get there, cementing the illusion that he had worked for a full hour. Eventually he showed up and stepped out into the alleyway to look around. He looked satisfied, even pleased.

Homeless: A Day in The Life.

"I guess you want to get paid now, eh?"

"Well, yeah. Nobody works for nothing, right?"

"I don't suppose you'd be willing to take some of our food instead, would you?"

Our friend could read the manager's mind, telling him he shouldn't give money to a homeless person, because they might spend it on alcohol. It was really just an excuse to be a cheapskate, and see how much he could bring the price down now that the work was done. If he could pay for it in trade instead of cash, all the better for him. Asshole.

"No sir, I'd rather not, and that's not the deal we made. You called the tune, and now you have to pay the piper. Besides, I think you're an honorable man, and you want to do what you said you would." If the manager insisted, that meant he was a dishonorable person; a cheat. And then he'd have an angry homeless man to deal with even though our friend had kept his cool.

"If you want to give me something to eat, I'll be happy to take it, and I won't let it go to waste, but you do your work to make money, and so do I." He made an effort to stay clear-headed and calm. The more lucid he was, the harder it would be for the boss to think of him as an alcoholic.

The manager sighed. He had to pay, and he knew it. There were stories about homeless people taking their revenge on small businesses by shitting in front of the entrance, or putting crazy glue in the store's locks. The homeless had very little protection under the law when they did casual labor, and they didn't resolve their disputes by taking people to court.

You could be hard on the homeless to an extent, but "even a dog will bark." The boss had just tried to be a prick, and now thought about how he could calm the situation down, even though it hadn't become an argument. He took out his wallet and handed over the $15.

"You know, you did a good job. If you're hungry, I'm sure we can find some food for you."

Just as he expected. "That'd be great. I could use a bite to eat." The manager, now dispensing charity, stepped back into the role of the alpha male. He was in command, and he made the decisions. Our friend would have no choice about what food they offered him. He knew better than to expect any.

The manager called into the restaurant, "Hey, Crispin, grab a "takeout" box, and give this guy something to eat. Whatever we have handy."

The man turned away with a smile and a nod, but didn't shake hands, the way people usually do when a business deal is completed. That implied he wasn't invited to come back, looking for more work. Of course, if he saw the same alley was a mess again later on, there was no reason why he couldn't bid on the job again. "No harm in asking."

The Mexican worker, Crispin, asked him, "What you want to eat, Sir?" pretending to show our friend the same respect he showed an ordinary customer. It was dignified for them both. For a moment, the dishwasher was promoted to something like a waiter, and our friend had been promoted to something like a customer. It felt good.

"I wanna make it easy for you, so whatever you got is fine, but I'm allergic to dairy products."

Our friend's street Spanish was pretty limited, but he knew how to say 'nothing made from milk'. "Nada hecho onde leche, por favor. Tengo un allergia." His Spanish was wrong, but comprehensible.

Crispin went back into the restaurant, and in a few minutes, came back with a chicken breast, a baked potato (with a pat of butter wrapped in aluminum foil), a bread roll, and some salad in a takeout box. The chicken and the potato had a brown sauce spread over it. Crispin even gave him a disposable fork and knife, in a plastic wrapper that also had a couple of napkins.

Our friend was very sure that Señor Crispin was giving him more than his boss would have liked. He was Mexican, and most of them grew up in a church that told its people to be compassionate. "That which you do to the least of my brethren, so you do unto me." Crispin had both a rosary and a scapular around his neck. The scapular insured that he'd go straight to heaven if he died suddenly.

It really was a full meal. He stopped being irritated at the manager for trying to connive him out of his wages. In fact, he guessed, if he had agreed to accept food instead of money, he probably would've got no better than the meal he was being given now. So, he won. Sort of.

"Muchas gracias. Usted un caballero." (Thank you. You are a gentleman).

Crispin told him, "You wait here one minute. I give you something more." In just a few seconds, he came back and handed him a can of Dr Pepper soda. Crispin really *was* a gentleman, and a son of Holy Mother Church.

He had a warm meal in his hands, and he knew it would be cold by the time he carried it back to the park, so he figured he'd stop for a moment, duck into a loading dock, and smoke a little more pot. After the effort of cleaning up behind the restaurant, he no longer felt anything from the last pot he'd smoked. It was a nice fresh "stone," and it felt really good. The ache in his back, from stooping over the ground in the alley, disappeared. He'd set up on the sidewalk after he took a hit.

He noticed that his pipe was starting to smell like pot, and he couldn't use it to smoke loose tobacco openly any longer. No problem. He'd find another way, and he had tobacco and rolling papers for now, and "now" was all that mattered. The sun had gone down well before he began to clean up the restaurant's alley, and the streets were getting quiet. He walked a couple of blocks toward the park until he came to an intersection with some remaining foot traffic. Some of the people walking by looked like tourists, and there were no other homeless people on that corner. It looked like a spot that might bring in something. He pulled a newspaper out of a trash barrel and sat down on it. He opened his backpack, took out his bowl, put a couple of coins in it, and put out his sign. "It's cold tonight (it was). Help me get a room."

Todd Murphy

CHAPTER EIGHT

Now that he was set up to panhandle while he ate, he started in on his food, with a silent prayer of thanksgiving, and a wordless blessing for Crispin, to the God he didn't really believe in, but who was handy to have around when he was in a prayerful mood. It seemed to happen more and more lately. Noticing himself and his own passing religious sentiment, he said a kind of grace over the food, as if it was going to do something for him. He didn't think it would, but it let him act the way he felt. Religion, the opium of the people, helped to dull his pain, too.

He noticed that the food was really excellent. The salad had some strange pink dressing on it that he didn't really care for, but he ate it anyway. It also had walnuts and pieces of cranberry in it, which he threw into the gutter. The flavor of cranberries was so sharp that he wondered if anyone actually liked them. But this was yuppie food, and they ate what they thought was healthy, even though they didn't like it very much. In his whole life, he'd never heard anyone saying that they really liked the taste of raw cranberries. Or kale. Whatever.

The chicken was cooked to perfection, and so was the baked potato. He wondered why there was no sour cream on it, a standard addition in expensive restaurants, and then remembered that he told Crispin that he couldn't eat anything made from milk. Most likely, Crispin had actually paid attention. Mexicans were *so* civilized, and he wondered for a moment if he might not be better off homeless in Mexico City. Probably not.

The meal was superb. He was stoned and enjoying the feeling of a full stomach. He chuckled at his own thought, "I should eat there more often." In fact, he did eat that kind of food regularly, taking leftovers from the trash, or claiming the "doggie bags" that people often left out in the street for the homeless. By the time he got to them, they were usually cold, and they never came with plastic forks and knives, or napkins. He finished his meal with a handful of the black jellybeans he'd found earlier in the day. This time, they had the sharp flavor he remembered from his childhood. Easter.

Nobody put anything in his bowl while he was eating. He didn't really expect it would bring in any money that time of day, but thinking with what passed for optimism, he said out loud, "you never know."

"You never know." Those words seemed to inform everything he did. The next person who walked by while he was panhandling. An unopened dumpster. The next trashcan. The next stretch of sidewalk, where he might find a little money on the ground. It happened. He was an unparalleled master of randomness, tempered by the ebb and flow of his luck. Luck and randomness were close colleagues, and together, they directed his days.

Stoned on his most recent hit of marijuana, he found himself thinking of two opposites at once. On the

Homeless: A Day in The Life.

one hand, homelessness was a prison. On the other, it was absolute freedom, so expansive that the normal points of reference that mark most people's days and lives didn't exist for him. Let other people think, "It's time to go to work" or "I have to stop at the grocery store on the way home to get some milk." These moments never happened for him, and the flow of time through his days had a rhythm that most people could never understand. He even got older more quickly than others. His real freedom consisted of doing what he had to, when he had to do it. "Freedom is the recognition of necessity."

On the other hand, letting his thoughts slide back and forth, he wasn't free to buy a snack without first counting his coins. He wasn't free to insist on his rights. He didn't have the freedom or the luxury to crawl into a bed at night, pull the blankets over himself, turn out the lights, and go to sleep. On the other hand (there was *always* an other hand); there was no alarm clock to wake him up at any specific time. He woke up to street noises, or the sound of an argument in the park where he slept. Sometimes, the police woke him up, but not to check his ID first thing in the morning. When there were a lot of tourists around, the cops liked to get the sleeping beggars up and out of the way before the sightseers hit the streets. Everything was fine as long as you did what the cops asked. That wasn't freedom, and America was supposed to be a free country. "Free means you don't have to pay." - Janis Joplin

There were times when he honestly couldn't decide whether it would be worth the long and painful struggle to try to repair his life; get a job and find an apartment. Then he'd go home to it each day after work, where he might put up his feet and watch movies "with all the digital quality of DVD." He remembered that these days it was Blu-Ray, and high definition. So what? Was a normal life *that* much better? Yes it was, but the equation that said so was far too complex for him to see its details.

He really *was* stoned. He noticed his own thoughts, and said to himself, "Woah!"

Another reality occurred to him, one that brought a lancing mental pain every time he thought of it. Even if he somehow returned to a normal life, he was too old, and his health too far gone for him to think that he could attract a woman. Without that motivation, he had less reason to try to repair himself. Sex and romantic love were simply outside of any reality he could imagine for himself.

There was a legend among the street people in the park. It told of a woman who went in there at night once in a while, and woke up the homeless men sleeping there to have sex with them, one after the other. It was probably nothing more than a story.

Doing that could get you busted for "public lewdness." The police just won't let you fuck in public whether it's day or night. In fact, any kind of sex among the homeless was against the law. You can't have sex outdoors in a public downtown park, under any circumstances whatsoever. Becoming homeless meant he had taken a kind of vow of celibacy before the law, even as he became ever more repugnant to most women. With no home to give them privacy, sex can get the homeless thrown in jail. A normal couple, having a tryst in a larger park, wouldn't be arrested. The cops would just tell them to go home and carry on.

> **Public lewdness:**
> "Knowingly engaging in any of the following acts in a public place or, if not in a public place, recklessness about whether another is present who will be offended or alarmed by the act of sexual intercourse; act of deviate sexual intercourse; act of sexual contact; or act involving contact between the person's mouth or genitals and the anus or genitals of an animal or fowl."

He doubted the legend of the woman who liked to fuck the homeless guys in the park was true, but even if it was, he was so tired all the time that he couldn't imagine himself fucking a strange woman after waking up in the middle of the night. Probably, that would change if he ever let go of the stress he lived with now. That was one really appealing thing about going back to a normal life. He'd be able to relax, and all the stress related disorders, problems, aches and pains he lived with would go away. But it was a distant dream, and "you can't get there from here." He thought he could become a new man and assumed that the new one would be better than the man he was now. He might even be able to visit his kid, and not feel like a dirty scumbag.

As the months and years on the street dragged on, he found he had fewer and fewer friends. His old friends from the time before his life fell apart no longer responded to him, so there was no help to be had from them. He didn't make many friends on the street. About half of them drank or took hard drugs, and were more trouble than their company was worth. They weren't homeless *because* they used drugs. They used drugs because they were homeless, and only the powerful intoxication of hard drugs or booze could relieve their stress. Soon after, they were addicted, and they didn't use them to feel good, they took them to stop feeling bad or to avoid feeling anything at all. Once they entered that cycle, there was really no escape without more pain than a street beggar is willing to take on. *Recovery* meant they were going to feel bad, no matter what they did. Our friend was glad marijuana was enough for him, and that he just didn't have a taste for alcohol or getting drunk. He'd have been dead by now.

He'd seen so many homeless people, some of them friends, simply disappear from the street and nobody knew what happened to them. A number of them had gone to jail. Some had returned to their families, to sleep in basements or garages while they looked for work. There were those who went into inpatient detox centers. Some died. Of these, some had killed themselves, but you didn't always find out who they were. One day, they were just gone.

He had been sitting there, his dinner finished, reflecting on his circumstances. Most of the time, that wasn't a very good thing to do. It left him depressed, and his pessimistic expectations always outweighed his hope for the future. His defeat wasn't absolute, because anything could happen at any time, good or bad. "You never know."

He decided he should walk back to the park, his home. Strange. He was actually thinking that he should "go home," even though he thought of it as a kind of safe zone more than a home. But that was okay; he was used to it, and that was enough. Maybe it *was* his home. Whatever.

He arrived there, surprised at how late it was, and made a mental note to himself to get a watch or a clock of some kind. It turned cold at night this time of year, and the only escape was to lay out his bed and go to sleep, but he wasn't quite ready for that.

He recalled that he'd found some vodka in the trash early that afternoon and resolved to remember to drink it just before he lay down. He might even get some extra sleep. It was only enough to help him stay warm, so he wouldn't have a hangover the next day. He didn't really like alcohol, but it was fine for sleep, because he wouldn't be awake to feel it.

He looked at the clock on one of the buildings. It was nearly midnight, and he had the choice between staying awake longer, and sleeping through the coldest part of the night, or going to sleep sooner, waking up at five or six in the morning, and feeling the early morning chill. He decided not to decide. He got out his marijuana, put a little more in his pipe, and smoked it, after first scanning for alien life forms; the police. There were none around, and the park was pretty quiet. The guys who stayed in one corner of the park with a boom box playing hip-hop music had gone home. "Silence is golden."

They were nice guys, all of them, and he'd never had any kind of argument with any of them, but they didn't seem to understand that some people really liked quiet. Once, they were there until about 2:30 in the morning, and he was forced to get up and try to find a doorway to sleep in. The police had stopped him a block away from the park, dragging his sleeping bag behind him, just to ask what he was doing that time of night. He told them how he usually slept in the park, but tonight it was too loud. The cop had said, "We have noise abatement laws here, so they really can't do that. That park is supposed to be quiet after 11 PM on weekdays, and 1 AM on the weekends." The police told him to stay warm, even though that was in the summer, and to watch himself on the street at night. This was advice he didn't need, because he'd already learned it many times over, but that's just the way the cops talk. They showed their compassion by giving advice. Sometimes they did the same thing to be intimidating. Whatever.

He didn't find an acceptable doorway, and so he walked in the other direction to look for one, passing by the park once again. Now, they hip-hop crowd was gone. He had made a complaint to the police about someone by mistake, and one of the cardinal unwritten rules of the street was that you never complained to the cops about anyone or anything. Ever. Ratting people out could get you beaten up or worse. Besides, he *believed* in that rule ("people who live in glass houses shouldn't throw stones"). He never would have said anything to the police if he knew they were going to hassle that distinguished convocation of most excellent gentlemen of the illustrious Afro-American persuasion.

Telling on people to the cops was something you just didn't do. He still felt a twinge of regret over that night. He lived within the law as much as he could, both the legal codes of the city, and the unwritten laws of the street. "Make no trouble; have no enemies."

He took out his book, and started to read by the icy light of the streetlamps. In fact, he didn't remember a word of what he'd read earlier, so he just started out again from the beginning. Reading was more important than what he read. Whatever.

Some time passed, and a few tourists milled about, staring off at the landscape in the distance. An Asian couple, acting like they were on their honeymoon, staged a selfie picture of themselves. A child, wearing made-in-China tennis shoes, with LEDs on its heels ran by, its parents sure they knew where their kid was. It was a quiet night, so far. The mood in the air was tranquil. There was no disturbance in the force.

Really, it had been a good day.

It was starting to cool down, and it was going to get *very* cold that night. He could feel it in the air. He closed up his book and tucked it into his backpack. There was a little more business to take care of before it was time for sleep. He walked up the street and turned into an alley, where he went behind a dumpster to piss, and then went behind another one, away from his own urine, opened his backpack and pulled out the newspaper he'd found earlier that day. He wished he'd remembered it when he was out sitting with his sign. He opened his pants, and keeping his long underwear in place, he wrapped his thighs in newspaper, and carefully raised them again to hold it in place, tucking it in as he went. Newspaper was a good insulator, but he had a warm sleeping bag, so he couldn't use too much or he'd get too hot. Crawling out of a sleeping bag, drenched in sweat that nearly froze in the night air made for a jarring moment. With his current gear, just wrapping his upper legs was enough. His coat stayed on.

Before he left the alley, he opened a recycling dumpster, and pulled out a couple of cardboard boxes. Of all the things he needed, empty cardboard boxes were the easiest to acquire. They were everywhere. The ones he needed, to go under his sleeping bag, was about 2' x 4', but that wasn't a very common size, and usually had to settle for one that was shorter than he liked. He didn't need to cushion his legs, but he was better off with a little padding under his torso. Two boxes, making four layers of cardboard, would be enough. It absorbs water too easily to be good insulation, but it only got soaked enough to turn cold when the ground was wet after a rain. The ones he found were good enough. He tucked them under his arm and went back to the park.

Feeling his body from within, he decided he didn't need to use a toilet again that night. That was one sensation you couldn't ignore, and it was difficult to deal with at 2:30 in the morning. You had to pack up everything, just to find a place to shit. If you left your things there, even for a few minutes, it might all be gone when you came back.

He made his way back to the park, stopping to fill his water bottle at the drinking fountain by the entrance.

He went back to the same place where he had been reading, laid down the cardboard, and spread out his sleeping bag on top of it. It had a camouflage pattern, so it blended in with the grass a little bit. That was ideal, because he didn't want to stand out or catch anyone's attention. It was easy to hide in plain sight when no one wanted to look at you, but you were always visible to the police and the drunken teenagers who liked to go "bum bashing." They were the reason why it was safer to sleep where everyone could see him, in a park with lots of police patrols.

He took off his shoes, and tied them to his backpack. Then, he set it down so its main flap was facing the ground. A thief would have to turn it over to open it, and they'd wake him up. He tucked his right arm into one of the shoulder straps, so he'd know if anyone tried to move it. At one time, he had a sleeping bag that would accommodate two people, and just brought his bag in with him, and he hoped he could find another. He took out the bottle of vodka, with its remaining two sips and drank it down, following it with another sip from his water bottle. Both went back in the backpack. He didn't want to leave the empty vodka bottle out where it could be seen.

"Public intoxication," and all that. It didn't take long to warm him up. He remembered the box of books waiting for him the next morning. He'd have to get to them first thing. They might not be there if he waited too long.

He felt his pocket to make sure his Service Medal was still there. It was right where it should be, it's purple metallic heart directly above his own.

A homeless man, sleeping in the street, doesn't turn off the light and roll over in his bed. Our friend's final ritual for the day was to pull a corner of the sleeping bag over his face to screen out the light from the streetlamps nearby. The day was done. He breathed deeply into the sleeping bag, to warm it with the heat from his breath and then, after a few minutes, he was asleep.

After some time, he couldn't tell how much, he felt something gently poking him in his ribs. He opened the sleeping bag to get a look at the situation, afraid it was a couple of "bum bashers." Instead, it was a pair of cops.

"Are you all right, sir?"

"Yeah, I'm fine. What's the trouble?"

"You sure you're alright?"

"Yes, sir. What's going on?"

"Nothing, sir. We're just doing a well-being check;

making sure everyone's okay. It's cold tonight." The cop offered him a silvery looking "space blanket," folded up so that it was only about 4 inches across. Actually, they were better than newspapers. "You can take this if you think you're going to be too cold."

Our friend reached out to take it, thanking the officer as he did so. "Thank you; I appreciate it." He could say "Thank you; I appreciate it" in his sleep; it was an automatic response from a man who got money by begging it from strangers.

The police walked away, looking for other homeless people to accept their space blankets.

A well-being check. He was well enough, he supposed.

He covered his face with the edge of his sleeping bag, wriggled his body to burrow in a little deeper, and said to himself:

"Jesus! It's fuckin' *cold*."

The End.

"A sample of 330 homeless adults were interviewed. Sixty-one percent of the study sample reported suicidal ideation and 34% had attempted suicide. Fifty-six percent of the men and 78% of the women reported prior suicidal ideation, while 28 percent of the men and 57% of the women had attempted suicide."

Eynan, R., Langley, J., Tolomiczenko, G., Rhodes, A.E., Links, P., Wasylenki, D. and Goering, P., 2002. "The association between homelessness and suicidal ideation and behaviors: results of a cross-sectional survey." *Suicide and Life-Threatening Behavior, 32*(4), pp.418-427.

Homeless: A Day in The Life.

ABOUT THE AUTHOR

The author, Todd Murphy, was homeless for about two and a half years, a long time before this book was written. As the years passed, he kept an interest in the lives of homeless people and the conditions they live in. Even though he eventually became a professional in neuroscience, he never stopped spending time with homeless people, or paying attention to how they lived. Murphy often answers questions about homelessness on Quora.com.

If you liked this book, please leave a review on Amazon.com. That's the best way to help others to find it, or to encourage the author to write more in this genre.

This book has an important message, and your review will help to spread it.

If you noticed any typos, please feel free to let the author know. To send your comments, please use the feedback form here:

https://tinyurl.com/homelessbook

---

[i] The DMV – "Department of motor vehicles," who issued all

drivers licenses and identification cards.

[ii] The Supplemental Nutrition Assistance Program card, which proved that someone was entitled to food stamps.

Made in the USA
San Bernardino, CA
30 December 2018